STEP-UP SKILLS FOR THE TOEIC® L&R TEST: Level 3 —Advanced— [2nd Edition]

Yasuyuki Kitao

Harumi Nishida

Shiho Hayashi

Brian Covert

Asahi Press

音声再生アプリ「リスニング・トレーナー」を使った音声ダウンロード

朝日出版社開発のアプリ、「リスニング・トレーナー（リストレ）」を使えば、教科書の音声をスマホ、タブレットに簡単にダウンロードできます。どうぞご活用ください。

◉ アプリ【リスニング・トレーナー】の使い方

《アプリのダウンロード》

App StoreまたはGoogle Playから「リスニング・トレーナー」のアプリ（無料）をダウンロード

App Storeはこちら▶

Google Playはこちら▶

《アプリの使い方》

① アプリを開き「コンテンツを追加」をタップ

② 画面上部に**【15721】**を入力しDoneをタップ

音声ストリーミング配信 》》》

この教科書の音声は、右記ウェブサイトにて無料で配信しています。

https://text.asahipress.com/free/english/

STEP-UP SKILLS FOR THE TOEIC® L&R TEST: Level 3 —Advanced— [2nd Edition]

協力
CPIジャパン
ナラボー・プレス
リント

はじめに

TOEIC® (Test of English for International Communication) テストは、「世界共通語としての英語によるコミュニケーション能力を測定するテスト」として、世界最大のテスト開発機関ETS (Educational Testing Service) によって開発され、1979年12月に第1回公開試験が実施されました。英語の聞く力・読む力・文法の知識を測るリスニングとリーディングを中心とする試験でしたが、2007年には英語を話す力・書く力を測るTOEIC® SPEAKING AND WRITING TESTSが始まり、今では英語の4技能（聞く・読む・話す・書く）の力を測ることができるテストになっています。またTOEIC®という名称は、以前は昔からあったリスニングとリーディングのテストを指していましたが、2016年8月からは、英語の聞く力・読む力を測るテストであるTOEIC® LISTENING AND READING TEST（略称：TOEIC® L&R）と、英語の話す力・書く力を測るTOEIC® SPEAKING AND WRITING TESTS（略称：TOEIC® S&W）の両方を指すテストブランド名として用いられることになりました。このことからも、TOEIC® テストは、英語の4技能を測るテストへと進化し続けていることがよく分かります。

今回の改訂版「Level 3 —Advanced—」は、『一歩上を目指すTOEIC® L&R』がシリーズ化されていなかった頃から数えると、2度目の改訂になります。今回の改訂版では、Part 1からPart 7まで、一部の問題を今の時代に即したトピックに置き換えるとともに、文法解説を充実させました。旧版と同様、単にTOEIC® L&Rのスコアを伸ばすことを目指すのではなく、TOEIC® L&R形式の問題演習を通して、英語を聞く力・読む力を総合的に伸ばし、かつ英文法の知識を身につけてもらうことを目指しています。

本テキストには、TOEIC® L&RのPart 1からPart 7の形式の問題に加えて、語彙問題（Vocabulary）、英語表現コラム（Useful Expression）、および文法解説（Grammar）といった「TOEIC＋α」の要素を盛り込んでいます。語彙問題は、日本語を介さずに英文から語彙を選ぶ方式にしています。これにより、文の中で語の意味を理解しながら語彙力をつけてもらうこと、および前後関係から意味を探り出す力を身につけることを目指しています。英語表現コラムは、基本的にそのユニットで出てくる英語表現を取り上げ、簡単な会話文とともにその表現を説明しています。会話文を暗唱するほど何度も声に出して読み、その表現の使い方を身につけてください。文法解説は、文法を公式として捉えるのではなく、テーマに挙げた文法項目の考え方を理解してもらうことを目指しています。解説を熟読し、例文を参考にして、英語の文に伴う文法の感覚を養ってほしいと思います。

本テキストを隅から隅まで活用していただくことにより、皆さんの英語の知識が増え、英語の聞く力・読む力が向上し、併せてTOEIC® L&Rのスコアが向上すれば、これに勝る喜びはありません。

本書を刊行するにあたっては、朝日出版社第一編集部の朝日英一郎様と鹿糖晟人様にたいへんお世話になりました。朝日様と鹿糖様のきめ細やかなご配慮および編集面からの的確なコメントにより、本テキストがより良いものになったことは間違いありません。また、他の編集部の皆様にも各段階でたいへんお世話になりました。ここに感謝申し上げます。

2023年10月

著者

本書について

本書の構成

本書は実際のTOEIC® LISTENING AND READING TEST（以下、TOEIC® L&Rと略）に準拠した問題とともに、語彙の練習問題および文法説明を設けています。TOEIC® L&R形式の問題を解くことに加えて、英語の力を伸ばすことを目標に据えています。
本書の構成は以下のとおりです。

◆**Vocabulary（語彙問題）**
各ユニットで出てくる重要語句を理解しましょう。

◆**TOEIC® L&R練習問題　Part 1: Photographs（写真描写問題）**
写真を見て英文を聞き、英語を聞く力を身につけましょう。

◆**TOEIC® L&R練習問題　Part 2: Question-Response（応答問題）**
文字情報に頼らず、音声情報だけで英語を聞き取れるようにしましょう。

◆**TOEIC® L&R練習問題　Part 3: Conversation（会話問題）**
会話をとおして英語を聞く力を身につけるとともに、会話でよく使われる表現を身につけましょう。

◆**TOEIC® L&R練習問題　Part 4: Talk（説明文問題）**
説明文を聞き、長い英語を聞き取れるようにしましょう。

◆**Useful Expression（英語表現コラム）**
よく使われる英語表現について、その英語表現を用いた会話文とともに説明しています。役立つ英語表現を覚えましょう。

◆**Grammar（文法説明）**
文法について、その考え方が詳しく書かれています。英語の構造についての理解を深めましょう。

◆**TOEIC® L&R練習問題　Part 5: Incomplete Sentences（短文穴埋め問題）**
文法問題をとおして、英語の文法や語彙の知識を増やしましょう。

◆**TOEIC® L&R練習問題　Part 6: Text Completion（長文穴埋め問題）**
長文空所補充問題をとおして、英語を読む力を身につけるとともに、文法や語彙の知識を増やしましょう。

◆**TOEIC® L&R練習問題　Part 7: Single Passage（1つの文書）/ Multiple Passages（複数の文書）**
様々な英文テキストを読み、問題に答えることで、英語の読解力を身につけましょう。

本書の使い方

本書はUnit 1からUnit 14まで14のテーマに基づいて問題が作られています。
TOEIC® L&R形式のリスニング練習問題（Part 1～Part 4）を解く前に、ボキャブラリーの問題を解いて語彙力の増強を図ってください。リスニング練習問題を解いた後は、英語表現コラム（Useful Expression）を読み、よく使われる英語表現についてそのニュアンスを会得してください。またTOEIC® L&R形式のリーディング練習問題（Part 5～Part 7）を解く前に、文法説明をよく読んで、英語の文法の知識を身につけるとともに、英語の感覚を身につけるよう心がけましょう。朝日出版社のウェブページには本テキストのリスニング問題の音声があります。こちらもダウンロードして、ぜひ活用してください（URLは、テキスト「はじめに」のページの前に載せています）。

TOEIC® LISTENING AND READING TESTの形式について

TOEIC® LISTENING AND READING TEST (TOEIC® L&R) は、リスニング問題100問（45分）、リーディング問題100問（75分）で構成されています。合否を判定するテストではなく、スコアにより評価されます。リスニング、リーディング各セクションが5点から495点の間でスコアとして算出され、2つのセクションを合計した、10点から990点の間でトータルスコアが算出されます。

TOEIC®を開発・製作しているEducational Testing Service（略称ETS）が、リスニング・リーディングのセクションごとに、スコア別に「長所」(Strength) と「短所」(Weakness) を記したレベル別評価の一覧表「Score Descriptor Table」を発表しています（https://www.ets.org/pdfs/toeic/toeic-listening-reading-score-descriptors.pdf）。日本でのTOEIC®の運営団体である「一般財団法人 国際ビジネスコミュニケーション協会」の公式ウェブページには、この評価一覧表を日本語に訳したものが挙げられています（https://www.iibc-global.org/toeic/test/lr/guide04/guide04_02/score_descriptor.html）。これらを自分の英語の力を測る目安として利用するとともに、スコアアップを目指す上での指針にするとよいでしょう。

TOEIC® L&Rは7つのパートに分かれています。そのうち4つのパートがリスニングで、3つのパートがリーディングです。リスニングではアメリカ・カナダ・イギリス・オーストラリア（ニュージーランドを含む）の英語が25%ずつ採用されています。各パートの問題形式および問題数は次のとおりです。

【リスニング セクション】

パート	内容	問題数
Part 1	**Photographs（写真描写問題）** 写真を見て、4つの説明文から写真の内容を最も的確に表現しているものを選びます。選択肢は印刷されていません。	6問
Part 2	**Question-Response（応答問題）** 質問文を聞いて、それに続く3つの応答から質問の答えとして合致しているものを選びます。質問文・応答とも印刷されていません。	25問
Part 3	**Conversations (with and without a visual image)（会話問題）** 2人もしくは3人で行われる会話に関連して出される設問に対して、適切な答えを選びます。1つの会話に対して、3つの質問が出されます。音声情報のみで答える問題もあれば、表やグラフ、地図などが付いた問題もあります。質問文も解答の選択肢もどちらも印刷されています。	39問 ［3問ずつ 13題］
Part 4	**Talks (with and without a visual image)（説明文問題）** 1人の話者によるアナウンスを聞き、そのアナウンスに関する質問に答えます。音声情報のみで答える問題もあれば、表やグラフ、地図などが付いた問題もあります。質問文、解答の選択肢、両方印刷されています。	30問 ［3問ずつ 10題］

【リーディング セクション】

パート	内容	問題数
Part 5	**Incomplete Sentences（短文穴埋め問題）** 短文の空所に当てはまる語句を4つの選択肢から選びます。 文法および語彙に関する問題が出題されます。	30問
Part 6	**Text Completion（長文穴埋め問題）** 1つの文章に対して、4つ穴埋めの問題があります。うち3つは単語や句を選ぶ問題で、文法的な見地や語彙の観点から問題が出されます。残り1つは文を補充する問題です。文脈を考えて、適切な文を選択肢より選びます。	16問 ［4問ずつ 4題］
Part 7	**Single Passage（1つの文書）、Multiple Passages（複数の文書）** 様々な英文テキストから問題が出されます。電子メールなどのテキストメッセージやチャットなど、複数の人物がやり取りしている文章もあります。それぞれのテキストに対して数問問題が出され、各々の質問に対して適切な答えを4つの選択肢から選びます。 1つの文章から問題が出されるSingle Passageの問題と、2つあるいは3つの文章から問題が出されるMultiple Passagesの問題の2つのタイプがあります。	29問 (single) 25問 (multiple)

TOEIC® LISTENING AND READING TESTの公開テストを受験するには、TOEIC® 公式ウェブページからのインターネット申し込みが必要です。詳しくは下記のTOEIC® 公式ウェブページをご覧ください。

●TOEIC® 公式ウェブページ（一般財団法人 国際ビジネスコミュニケーション協会）
https://www.iibc-global.org/toeic.html

同ウェブページによると、本テキスト執筆時で最新のデータである2022年度のTOEIC® L&Rの受験者数は、公開テスト受験者が97万人、団体特別受験制度による受験者が100万1千人の計197万1千人でした。

TOEIC® Programについて

現在、TOEIC® Programには、以下のテストがあります。

TOEIC® Tests

・TOEIC® LISTENING AND READING TEST

英語を聞く力、読む力、および英文法の知識を測るテストです。

＜テスト形式＞ マークシートによる一斉客観テスト
＜テスト時間＞ 120分（リスニング45分、リーディング75分）
＜テスト結果＞ リスニング5～495点、リーディング5～495点、
合計10～990点
（スコアは5点刻みで算出されます。）

・TOEIC® SPEAKING AND WRITING TESTS

英語を話す力および書く力を測るテストです。

＜テスト形式＞ テスト会場にてパソコンを使用して実施
＜テスト時間＞ スピーキング20分、ライティング60分
＜テスト結果＞ スピーキング0～200点、ライティング0～200点、
（スコアは10点刻みで算出されます。）
※スピーキングのみ、ライティングのみの受験も可能です。

TOEIC Bridge® Tests

・TOEIC Bridge® Listening & Reading Tests

TOEIC® LISTEING AND READING TEST (TOEIC® L&R) よりも易しいレベルのテストで、英語を聞く力、読む力、および英文法の知識を測るテストです。

＜テスト形式＞ マークシートによる一斉客観テスト
＜テスト時間＞ 60分（リスニング25分、リーディング35分）
＜テスト結果＞ リスニング15～50点、リーディング15～50点、
合計30～100点
（スコアは1点刻みで算出されます。）

・TOEIC Bridge® Speaking & Writing Tests

TOEIC® SPEAKING AND WRITING TESTS (TOEIC® S&W) よりも易しいレベルのテストで、英語を話す力および書く力を測るテストです。

＜テスト形式＞ テスト会場にてパソコンを使用して実施
＜テスト時間＞ 52分（スピーキング15分、ライティング37分）
＜テスト結果＞ スピーキング15～50点、ライティング15～50点、
合計30～100点
（スコアは1点刻みで算出されます。）
※IPテストの場合は、スピーキングのみ、ライティングのみの受験も可能です。

詳しくは、TOEIC® 公式ウェブページをご覧ください。

Contents

STEP-UP SKILLS FOR THE TOEIC®
L&R TEST: Level 3 —Advanced— [2nd Edition]

Unit 1 Eating Out

Warm-up

Vocabulary

空欄に下から適切な語句を選んで書き入れなさい。なお、動詞については原形で記されています。必要に応じて適切な形に変えなさい。

1. You should try the clam chowder, since it is the local (　　　　　　).
2. If you bring a coupon, all children's dishes will be 10 percent off the (　　　　　　).
3. Our (　　　　　　) is a staffing agency that sends personnel to restaurants, cafés and bars.
4. The discount coupons will (　　　　　　) tomorrow, so hurry up and use them.
5. You should (　　　　　　) because this café is always crowded.
6. Please (　　　　　　) the reservation desk when the number of people is fixed.

firm	specialty	make a reservation
contact	expire	regular price

TOEIC® Listening

Part 1 Photographs

You will hear four short statements. Look at the picture and choose the statement that best describes what you see in the picture.

1.

Ⓐ Ⓑ Ⓒ Ⓓ

2.

Ⓐ Ⓑ Ⓒ Ⓓ

03

You will hear a question or statement and three responses. Listen carefully, and choose the best response to the question or statement.

3. Mark your answer on your answer sheet. Ⓐ Ⓑ Ⓒ

4. Mark your answer on your answer sheet. Ⓐ Ⓑ Ⓒ

5. Mark your answer on your answer sheet. Ⓐ Ⓑ Ⓒ

6. Mark your answer on your answer sheet. Ⓐ Ⓑ Ⓒ

04

You will hear a short conversation between two or more people. Listen carefully, and select the best response to each question.

7. Why is the restaurant closed?
(A) For renewal
(B) Due to a labor shortage
(C) To move to a different location
(D) To make a new website for the restaurant Ⓐ Ⓑ Ⓒ Ⓓ

8. How did the speaker get the information about the reopening?
(A) The restaurant's website
(B) A notice
(C) From a friend
(D) From the restaurant's staff Ⓐ Ⓑ Ⓒ Ⓓ

9. When will they probably come back to the restaurant?
(A) On Tuesday next week
(B) On Friday this week
(C) On Tuesday this week
(D) On Saturday next week Ⓐ Ⓑ Ⓒ Ⓓ

05

You will hear a short talk given by a single speaker. Listen carefully, and select the best response to each question.

10. What is cheaper than usual?

(A) Ginger ale
(B) Steak
(C) Beer
(D) Wine

Ⓐ Ⓑ  

11. What does the speaker mention about the restaurant?

(A) It has just opened.
(B) It is open for tonight only.
(C) Takeout is available.
(D) Catering is available.

Ⓐ Ⓑ  

12. What does the man say about their popular dishes?

(A) Nothing is left now.
(B) They will probably be sold out soon.
(C) They are ready-made meals.
(D) Some are 20 dollars off.

Ⓐ Ⓑ  

Useful Expression

Let's have a bite.

「ちょっと軽く食べよう」という表現です。この "bite" はもともと「ひとくち、ひとかじり」という意味ですが、もちろんひとくちだけ食べるというわけではありません。「ひとくち、ひとかじり」から転じて「軽食」という意味が出てきました。

A: Let's have a bite before the flight. I'm not sure when we'll be able to eat in the plane.
(フライトの前に軽く食べよう。飛行機の中ではいつ食べられるか分からないからね。)

B: That's a good idea! Then, how about a sandwich? There's a nice sandwich bar over there.
(それはいい考えだ。じゃあ、サンドイッチはどうだい。あそこにいいサンドイッチの店があるんだ。)

なお、このようにbiteはhave a biteの形で用いられ、eat a biteとは言いません。「食べる」ことをはっきり表すeatではなくhaveを使うところからも、「軽く食べる」というニュアンスが出ていますね。

Grammar

動詞（1）

<例文> (i) We leave Boston at 9 a.m. and arrive in New York at 1 p.m.
(ii) We are leaving Boston tonight.

動詞の時制には、出来事をどのように捉えているかという視点が反映されています。その視点を押さえることが、動詞の時制の理解につながります。例文 (i) と (ii) にはどのようなニュアンスの差があるのでしょうか。

(i) は現在形で、(ii) は現在進行形になっています。現在形は基本的には動詞が表す出来事全体に目が向けられ、その出来事を「恒常的に（いつも）」行っているというニュアンスがあるのに対して、現在進行形は動詞が表わす出来事のうちの一部が「いま進行中」であることを示します。よって、(i) は例えばツアーを組んでいる旅行会社が旅行行程表などに書いた文句であると言えるでしょう。つまりいつもこのような行程でツアーが行われていることを説明した文だと言えます。(ii) はなぜ「現在」進行形がtonightという「未来」を表わす語句と結びつくかと言えば、現在進行形のニュアンスに照らし合わせば、「ボストンを去る」という行為の一部がいま行われているということで、例えばチケットを購入するといった手配ができており、今夜ボストンを去る準備が着々と進んでいることを含意していると言えます。よって未来の出来事について言っている文ですが、現在進行形を使うことができます。このことから、現在進行形を用いて未来のことを述べているときは、比較的近い未来のこと、そしてその動作が意図的にできることを示しています。例えばいくら近い未来のことでも、"It is raining tomorrow." というのは少し不自然です。なぜなら、この文を発した人が意図的に雨を降らすことができないからです。空を見て雨が降りそうだということで、"It is going to rain tomorrow." と言うことは可能です。

このように出来事の捉え方と時制は強く結びついていることが分かります。英文にたくさん触れ、その感覚を少しずつ身につけていきましょう。

TOEIC® Reading

Part 5 Incomplete Sentences

A word or phrase is missing in each of the sentences below. Select the best answer to complete the sentence.

13. The fee that the art school charges for its classes __________ the cost of materials.

(A) including (B) included
(C) include (D) includes

14. The bus-stop sign stated that the shuttle __________ making four stops before arriving at the City Air Terminal.

(A) will do　(B) would be
(C) have been　(D) was to

Ⓐ Ⓑ Ⓒ Ⓓ

15. The company will reduce advertising costs, as the campaign __________ in two weeks' time.

(A) would have expired　(B) is going to expire
(C) was expiring　(D) has expired

Ⓐ Ⓑ Ⓒ Ⓓ

16. Ms. Martin __________ in the same office on the fourth floor ever since she joined the firm 12 years ago.

(A) works　(B) is working
(C) has worked　(D) would work

Ⓐ Ⓑ Ⓒ Ⓓ

17. Until last year's sudden increase in the cost of gasoline, Mercrom Motors' newest sports car __________ well.

(A) has been selling　(B) has been sold
(C) had been selling　(D) will have sold

Ⓐ Ⓑ Ⓒ Ⓓ

18. Mr. Keenan and Ms. Smith __________ to work together on the Internet retailing project.

(A) assigning　(B) will assign
(C) assigned　(D) have been assigned

Ⓐ Ⓑ Ⓒ Ⓓ

19. Please __________ the plant manager before using any machinery connected to the computer.

(A) contact　(B) contacting
(C) have contacted　(D) contacted

Ⓐ Ⓑ Ⓒ Ⓓ

20. Tim McCawley is planning to pick up his client when she __________ at Toronto Pearson Airport.

(A) arrives　(B) arrived
(C) arriving　(D) will arrive

Ⓐ Ⓑ Ⓒ Ⓓ

Part 6 Text Completion

Read the text that follows. A word, phrase, or sentence is missing in parts of the text. Select the best answer to complete the text.

Questions 21-24 refer to the following notice.

> ***To all members of the Waterford Country Club:***
>
> On Saturdays, Sundays and holidays, reservations for the country club's main dining room are a must. You can make your reservation by phone, online or by stopping by the reception desk at the club -------.
> **21.**
>
> Please remember, the main dining room enforces a dress code during the dinner hours, 5:00 until closing.
> Snacks and drinks are available for your enjoyment in the café by the pool. Reservations are not required and dress is -------. -------.
> **22.** **23.**
>
> In addition to our main dining room and café, our banquet service can accommodate private groups from 10 to 400 for informal and formal occasions. Consult the food service manager for prices and scheduling. The club's food service ------- provides catering for events that are not held here at Waterford
> **24.**
> Country Club.

21. (A) service
(B) entrance
(C) opening
(D) schedule

Ⓐ Ⓑ Ⓒ Ⓓ

22. (A) casually
(B) casual work
(C) casualness
(D) casual

Ⓐ Ⓑ Ⓒ Ⓓ

23. (A) You should call the café and reserve a seat before you go there.
(B) We believe that you can enjoy a buffet dinner at the café.
(C) Internet cafés have developed along with the spread of the Internet itself.
(D) The café is open at all times while the club is open from 10:00 a.m. to 10:00 p.m.

Ⓐ Ⓑ Ⓒ Ⓓ

24. (A) even
(B) because
(C) unless
(D) although

Ⓐ Ⓑ Ⓒ Ⓓ

Read the following text. Select the best answer for each question.

Questions 25-28 refer to the following survey.

❀ Mayberry Garden Bistro ❀

Dear Valued Customers:

We at Mayberry Garden Bistro care deeply about the quality of our services. Please take just a few moments to fill out the following questionnaire to help us make your dining experience here even better in the future.

	Excellent	Good	Fair	Poor
Reservations				
Hostess		✓		
Server			✓	
Timeliness of service			✓	
Quality of food		✓		
Cleanliness			✓	
Interior	✓			
Bar				

Would you visit our Bistro again? ☑ Yes ☐ No

Please do give us your comments!

Our server was really friendly, but it took a little long to get our meal after we ordered. Our table was also a bit messy when we arrived. It had not yet been cleaned and it remained dirty for about 15 minutes after we sat down.

The strawberry shortcake was the best ever, though! Thank you.

25. Why does Mayberry Garden produce a questionnaire?

(A) To survey employee satisfaction
(B) To keep up their good service
(C) To hire excellent staff
(D) To maintain good relations with management

Ⓐ Ⓑ Ⓒ Ⓓ

26. What is mentioned about the service?

(A) It was very speedy and efficient.
(B) The waitress did not smile enough.
(C) The order was incorrectly placed.
(D) The table had not been prepared in time.

Ⓐ Ⓑ Ⓒ Ⓓ

27. How does the customer evaluate the design of the Bistro?

(A) Excellent
(B) Good
(C) Fair
(D) Poor

Ⓐ Ⓑ Ⓒ Ⓓ

28. With what was the customer very satisfied?

(A) Dessert
(B) Cocktails
(C) The main course
(D) Appetizers

Ⓐ Ⓑ Ⓒ Ⓓ

Unit 2 Travel

Warm-up

Vocabulary

空欄に下から適切な語句を選んで書き入れなさい。なお、動詞については原形で記されています。必要に応じて適切な形に変えなさい。

1. I preferred an (　　　　　　　), but my airline company says they are fully booked.
2. I got an (　　　　　　　) this morning for the next business trip.
3. The (　　　　　　　) says we need visas to visit the sightseeing spots.
4. All employees have to (　　　　　　　) our supervisor when they travel overseas.
5. The local Hawaii (　　　　　　　) of World Travel Co. prepares many optional tours for young children.
6. Your suitcase was a bit damaged during the flight, so the airline company will (　　　　　　　) you for that.

itinerary	travel agent	compensate
notify	aisle seat	branch

TOEIC® Listening

Part 1 Photographs

06

You will hear four short statements. Look at the picture and choose the statement that best describes what you see in the picture.

1.

Ⓐ Ⓑ Ⓒ Ⓓ

2.

Ⓐ Ⓑ Ⓒ Ⓓ

Part 2 Question-Response

07

You will hear a question or statement and three responses. Listen carefully, and choose the best response to the question or statement.

3. Mark your answer on your answer sheet. Ⓐ Ⓑ Ⓒ

4. Mark your answer on your answer sheet. Ⓐ Ⓑ Ⓒ

5. Mark your answer on your answer sheet. Ⓐ Ⓑ Ⓒ

6. Mark your answer on your answer sheet. Ⓐ Ⓑ Ⓒ

Part 3 Conversation

08

You will hear a short conversation between two or more people. Listen carefully, and select the best response to each question.

7. When did they get the detailed information for the trip?
(A) The 23rd
(B) 10 a.m.
(C) Last week
(D) Yesterday
Ⓐ Ⓑ Ⓒ Ⓓ

8. How will they probably get to the hotel?
(A) By cab
(B) By air
(C) By bus
(D) On foot
Ⓐ Ⓑ Ⓒ Ⓓ

9. What are they worrying about?
(A) Departure time
(B) Arrival time
(C) Location of the hotel
(D) Sleeping hours
Ⓐ Ⓑ Ⓒ Ⓓ

You will hear a short talk given by a single speaker. Listen carefully, and select the best response to each question.

10. Who most likely is the speaker?

(A) A visitor
(B) A park official
(C) A tour guide
(D) A vet

Ⓐ Ⓑ Ⓒ Ⓓ

11. Look at the graphic. Which trail is NOT taken for this tour?

(A) North Trail
(B) South Trail
(C) Colorado Trail
(D) None of the above

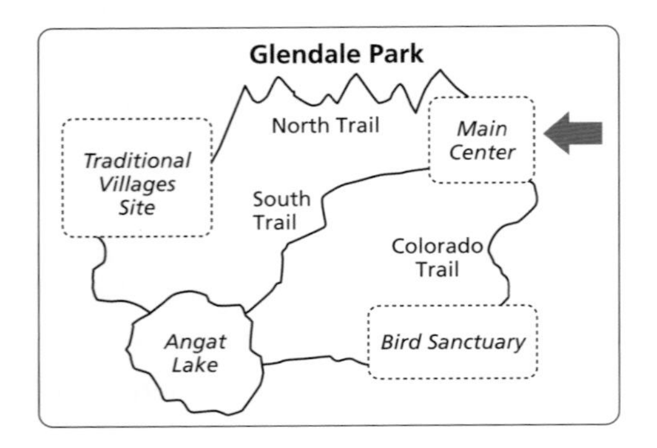

12. What does the woman suggest to the listeners?

(A) To take a map
(B) To check the weather
(C) To wear sunscreen
(D) To stay well hydrated

Ⓐ Ⓑ Ⓒ Ⓓ

Useful Expression

Either is OK with me.

「私はどちらでも構いません」という言い方です。either A or B（AかBのどちらか）の慣用句と関連づけて、「片一方はいいのですが...」と勘違いする人もいるようです。eitherはもともと選択肢を2つに絞って、その中の1つを示す言い方です。either A or Bの場合はorを使ってはっきりと2つの選択肢（AとB）を示して、このAかBのどちらかという意味になります。Either is OK with me. の場合も2つの選択肢のうち「どちらか一つ」なのですが、すでに会話の中に出てきたA, Bという選択肢を頭に描き、Aを選んでもBを選んでもどちらでも構わないということを示しています。よって、either A or Bのeitherも、Either is OK with me. のeitherも、意味は同じと言えます。

A: Would you like to eat a hamburger or a chicken burrito?
（ハンバーガーか、チキンブリトーを食べないかい。）

B: Either is OK with me. I really like both of them.
（どっちでもいいよ。どちらも好きだからね。）

Grammar

動詞 (2)

＜例文＞ (i) I <u>went</u> to Budapest.
(ii) I <u>have been</u> to Budapest.

日本語と英語は時制の捉え方が異なります。英語の時制の概念を身につけることは、英語の感覚を養う上で重要です。例文 (i) では過去形が使われ、例文 (ii) では現在完了形が使われていますが、両者はどのような違いがあるのでしょうか。

過去形は、「行動そのもの」に焦点が当たっています。また、現在から過去を見て、その出来事を「点」として捉えています。

【過去形】

went to Budapest　　現在

それに対して、現在完了形は、どちらかというと、過去の出来事の「結果」に焦点を当てています。その出来事の結果が現在にも及んでいる。つまり、出来事があった時点から現在までの影響を「帯」として捉えています。

【現在完了形】

have been to Budapest　現在

よって、例文 (i) の場合は、過去の「ブダペストに行った」という事実そのものを振り返って「点」で表すようなイメージで捉えているのに対し、例文 (ii) はブダペストに行った時点から現在までを経験として「帯」のように捉えていることから、「ブダペストに行ったことがある」という意味になります。

このことから、過去形は「点」で表せるような要素と結び付けることができますが、現在完了形はそのような要素とは結び付けることができません。

＜例文＞ (iii) ○ I lived in Manila last year.
(iv) × I have lived in Manila last year.
(v) ○ I have lived in Manila for five years.

例文 (iii) は過去形 (lived) が使われており、現在から振り返って昨年の出来事を「点」の形で表しています。例文 (iv) は現在完了形 (have lived) ですので、「点」の要素の last year とは結び付けられません。現在完了形は、例文 (v) のように、過去のある時点ではなく、今から振り返って「マニラに5年間住んでいた」(for five years) という「帯」のような形で示すことができる要素と一緒に用いることができます。

ちなみに、例文 (vi) の used to は、「過去のある時点までずっとやっていたけれど、今はやっていない」という意味を含みます。すなわち、過去に「帯」の形で捉える出来事があるのですが、この帯が現在まで伸びていません。

＜例文＞ (vi) I used to play the piano. (昔はよくピアノを弾いていました。)

TOEIC® Reading

Part 5 Incomplete Sentences

A word or phrase is missing in each of the sentences below. Select the best answer to complete the sentence.

13. The closure of our factories for repairs __________ in a sharp decrease in our quarterly production figures.

(A) to result (B) have resulted
(C) has resulted (D) resulting

Ⓐ Ⓑ Ⓒ Ⓓ

14. The maintenance work __________ between the hours of 10 p.m. and 6 a.m., when the offices are closed for the night.

(A) conduct (B) conducting
(C) is conducted (D) has conducted

Ⓐ Ⓑ Ⓒ Ⓓ

15. Mr. Lee __________ your project proposal by the time you come here tomorrow.

(A) will read (B) will have read
(C) have read (D) is reading

Ⓐ Ⓑ Ⓒ Ⓓ

16. The atmosphere in the campaign __________ now that the election is drawing close.

(A) is intensifying (B) was intensifying
(C) intensifying (D) have intensified

Ⓐ Ⓑ Ⓒ Ⓓ

17. Seldom did she __________ branches outside Japan last year, but she has to go to one of the branches at least once a year.

(A) visit (B) visited
(C) visits (D) has visited

Ⓐ Ⓑ Ⓒ Ⓓ

18. The electronics store refused to repair the computer for free because the warranty __________ already.

(A) expires (B) expired
(C) had expired (D) will expire

Ⓐ Ⓑ Ⓒ Ⓓ

19. As the company's business increased, more and more people were hired to __________ care of the additional work.

(A) be taken (B) took
(C) take (D) have taken

Ⓐ Ⓑ Ⓒ Ⓓ

20. If there are any changes to the seminar schedule, all speakers will __________ at least a week in advance.

(A) notify (B) be notifying
(C) have notified (D) be notified

Ⓐ Ⓑ Ⓒ Ⓓ

Part 6 Text Completion

Read the text that follows. A word, phrase, or sentence is missing in parts of the text. Select the best answer to complete the text.

Questions 21-24 refer to the following letter.

Mr. Felix Markowitz
8282 Heatherton Way
Durham, NC 29807

Dear Mr. Markowitz:

We have reviewed your letter regarding the difficulty you experienced at Port Vale on your recent trip to Bermuda.

We value your patronage and hope that you will continue to use our agency for your travel needs. _______ (**21.**), we would like to offer you a credit voucher in the amount of $75 that can be applied toward your next travel booking with us. Please accept the enclosed voucher with our apologies as a _______ (**22.**) of compensating you for the inconvenience you endured. This is, of course, in addition to the refund of $115 for the boat tour which _______ (**23.**) for you. We are very sorry that we did not notify you of the cancellation and that you had to find out about it only after you arrived at the docks. _______ (**24.**).

Sincerely,

Marsh Phelps
Getaway Travel Agency

21. (A) Therefore
(B) However
(C) Otherwise
(D) Eventually

Ⓐ Ⓑ Ⓒ Ⓓ

22. (A) mean
(B) means
(C) meaning
(D) meaningful

Ⓐ Ⓑ Ⓒ Ⓓ

23. (A) had arranged
(B) to be arranged
(C) had been arranged
(D) will be arranging

Ⓐ Ⓑ Ⓒ Ⓓ

24. (A) Once again, we offer our deepest apologies.
(B) You are required to submit your proposal within the next 20 days.
(C) We will tell you how much we can refund to you.
(D) Our company has started a route between Port Vale and Bermuda.

Ⓐ Ⓑ Ⓒ Ⓓ

Part 7 Single Passage

Read the following text. Select the best answer for each question.

Questions 25-28 refer to the following itinerary.

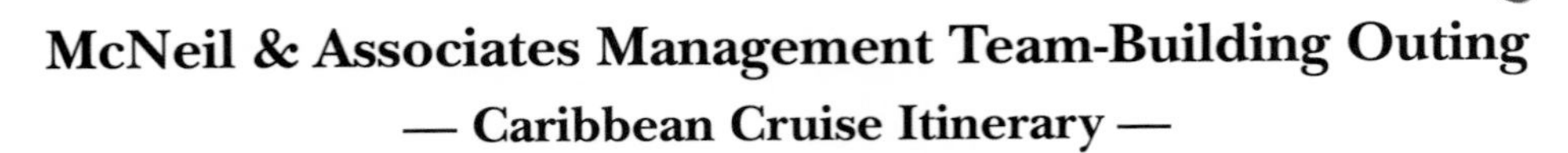

McNeil & Associates Management Team-Building Outing

— Caribbean Cruise Itinerary —

TUESDAY, JUNE 26

Morning: Board ship in Miami

Afternoon: Free time

Evening: Team-building activities (recreation area – main deck)

WEDNESDAY, JUNE 27

Morning: Group breakfast

Afternoon: Arrive in Ocho Rios, Jamaica

Evening: Dinner in Ocho Rios, Jamaica

THURSDAY, JUNE 28

Morning: Free time

Afternoon: Onshore group activities — rafting, hiking

Evening: Dinner in Ocho Rios. Set Sail for Georgetown, Grand Cayman

FRIDAY, JUNE 29

Morning: Arrive in Georgetown, Grand Cayman

Afternoon: Snorkeling, scuba diving

Evening: Free time. Set sail for Miami

SATURDAY, JUNE 30

Morning: Team-building activities (3rd floor conference room)

Afternoon: Feedback and wrap-up conference

Evening: Arrive in Miami

25. What is the Caribbean Cruise planned for?

(A) To train new company employees
(B) To attend a conference in Jamaica
(C) To enjoy marine sports
(D) To promote team-building in a company

Ⓐ Ⓑ Ⓒ Ⓓ

26. Which activity will take place in Ocho Rios?

(A) A management meeting
(B) A hiking trip
(C) A group breakfast
(D) Snorkeling

Ⓐ Ⓑ Ⓒ Ⓓ

27. How many times will they have free time?

(A) Once
(B) Twice
(C) Three times
(D) Four times

Ⓐ Ⓑ Ⓒ Ⓓ

28. Where in the ship will they have the second team-building activities?

(A) In a recreation area
(B) In a conference room
(C) In a business center
(D) In a large dining room

Ⓐ Ⓑ Ⓒ Ⓓ

Unit 3 Amusement

Warm-up

Vocabulary

空欄に下から適切な語を選んで書き入れなさい。なお、動詞については原形で記されています。必要に応じて適切な形に変えなさい。

1. The musical was so popular that there were very few (　　　　　　) seats at the theater.
2. The concert hall was fully (　　　　　　) with young people.
3. My brother has (　　　　　　) movie tickets on the Internet for me.
4. Please (　　　　　　) a budget plan for the annual art exhibition by next Monday.
5. We are planning to open new (　　　　　　) for sports and recreation by the end of this year.
6. The amusement park (　　　　　　) free limousine bus service from the nearest train station.

empty	offer	submit
occupy	book	facilities

TOEIC® Listening

Part 1 Photographs

10

You will hear four short statements. Look at the picture and choose the statement that best describes what you see in the picture.

1.

Ⓐ Ⓑ Ⓒ Ⓓ

2.

Ⓐ Ⓑ Ⓒ Ⓓ

Part 2 Question-Response 11

You will hear a question or statement and three responses. Listen carefully, and choose the best response to the question or statement.

3. Mark your answer on your answer sheet. Ⓐ Ⓑ Ⓒ

4. Mark your answer on your answer sheet. Ⓐ Ⓑ Ⓒ

5. Mark your answer on your answer sheet. Ⓐ Ⓑ Ⓒ

6. Mark your answer on your answer sheet. Ⓐ Ⓑ Ⓒ

Part 3 Conversation 12

You will hear a short conversation between two or more people. Listen carefully, and select the best response to each question.

7. What are the speakers mainly talking about?
- (A) Gallery renovation
- (B) Tickets for an art exhibition
- (C) Refundable tickets
- (D) Plans for an upcoming trip

Ⓐ Ⓑ Ⓒ Ⓓ

8. Why does the second woman not take the tickets?
- (A) She wants to travel alone.
- (B) She needs to change her ticket.
- (C) She already bought some of her own.
- (D) She wants to know how to get a ticket.

Ⓐ Ⓑ Ⓒ Ⓓ

9. Why does the man think it is a coincidence?
- (A) Because he went to the exhibition with his wife
- (B) Because the others are talking about the tickets which he needs
- (C) Because he got a special discount for the tickets
- (D) Because he and his wife are looking forward to the show

Ⓐ Ⓑ Ⓒ Ⓓ

You will hear a short talk given by a single speaker. Listen carefully, and select the best response to each question.

10. What is it that people CANNOT enjoy?

(A) Dance (B) Food and drink
(C) Shopping (D) Live music

Ⓐ Ⓑ Ⓒ Ⓓ

11. How many days does the event last?

(A) One hundred days (B) Six days
(C) Five days (D) Two days

Ⓐ Ⓑ Ⓒ Ⓓ

12. What is mentioned about the event?

(A) It is for adults only.
(B) The location has changed.
(C) Entrance fee is not required.
(D) There will be a dance competition.

Ⓐ Ⓑ Ⓒ Ⓓ

Useful Expression

That sounds like fun.

「それは楽しそうだ」という言い方です。このsoundは動詞で、「（聞いてみると）～のように思われる」という意味を表します。That sounds like fun.の場合は、相手の言葉を聞いて、「それは（聞いてみると）楽しそうに思われる」ということから、「それは楽しそうだ」という意味になります。

A: Are you interested in the Sydney tour that Northtale Travel Agency offers? We can try hang-gliding on the tour.
（ノーステール旅行代理店がやっているシドニーツアーに興味あるかい。ツアーでハンググライダーに挑戦できるよ。）

B: That sounds like fun. Let's sign up for it right now!
（それは楽しそうだね。今すぐ申し込もうよ。）

funは名詞なので、sound like funのようにlikeを伴いますが、"(That) sounds strange."（おかしいなぁ）、"(That) sounds difficult."（難しそうだなぁ）のように、形容詞が使われる場合は、動詞soundはすぐ後に形容詞を取ります。このように「～のように思われる」の意味を表すsoundは ＜sound + 形容詞＞ または ＜sound like + 名詞＞ の形で用いられます。

Grammar

品詞

<例文> (i) ○ They quarreled with each other in a loud voice.
(ii) × They quarreled with each other in a loudly voice.

品詞の概念を知っておくことは、英語を理解する上で重要です。例えば、onlyやjustのような例外はありますが、基本的には副詞は名詞を修飾できません。よって、名詞を修飾できる形容詞 (loud) が名詞 (voice) の前に置かれている (i) は正しいですが、副詞 (loudly) が名詞 (voice) を修飾している (ii) は間違いとなります。

TOEIC® L&Rの問題では、空所の前後をよく見ることが大切です。次の例題を解きましょう。

<例題> 次の空所に当てはまる語句を記号で選びなさい。

① I heard that the ________ sisters of the mayor will debut in a movie.
(A) beauty (B) beautiful (C) beautifully (D) beauties

② I had ________ fun going around Los Angeles.
(A) a lot of (B) most (C) very (D) so

例題 ① は、空所の前にtheがあるので、冠詞は名詞の前につけられることから (A) beauty を選んだ人もいるかもしれませんが、答えは (B) beautiful です。後ろにsistersという名詞があるため、冠詞theと名詞sistersの間に入ることができるのは、名詞を修飾する形容詞ということになります。

例題 ② は、日本語と英語では品詞の扱いが異なることに注意する必要があります。日本語に訳すと「ロサンゼルスをあちこち回って楽しかった」となり、「楽しい」という形容詞が使われているため、英語のfunも形容詞だと考え、形容詞を修飾できる副詞である (C) veryを選んでしまったかもしれませんが、答えは (A) a lot ofです。英語の "fun" は名詞であるため、副詞のveryは名詞funを修飾できません。funが名詞であることは、hadの目的語になっていることからも分かります。このように、日本語の感覚に引っ張られてしまわないようにすることが大切です。ちなみにfunは、くだけた言い方では "It was a fun evening." のように形容詞としても用いられますが、基本的には名詞として使われます。

(例題解答・訳)
① B (私は、市長の美しい姉妹が映画でデビューすると聞きました。)
② A (私は、ロサンゼルスをあちこち回ってとても楽しかったです。)

TOEIC® Reading

Part 5 Incomplete Sentences

A word or phrase is missing in each of the sentences below. Select the best answer to complete the sentence.

13. The Italian restaurant on 5th Street is __________ popular among young people.
(A) wideness (B) widen
(C) wide (D) widely
Ⓐ Ⓑ Ⓒ Ⓓ

14. At the __________ of the CEO, the division manager will be promoted to vice president next year.
(A) suggestion (B) suggestive
(C) suggestively (D) suggest
Ⓐ Ⓑ Ⓒ Ⓓ

15. The machinery of the production line was __________ checked out before starting the operation.
(A) through (B) thorough
(C) thoroughly (D) thoroughness
Ⓐ Ⓑ Ⓒ Ⓓ

16. Each project proposal must be submitted quickly and __________ in writing.
(A) accurate (B) accurately
(C) accuracy (D) accurateness
Ⓐ Ⓑ Ⓒ Ⓓ

17. The management is considering the cutting of labor costs, but the __________ decision has not yet been made.
(A) finale (B) finalize
(C) final (D) finally
Ⓐ Ⓑ Ⓒ Ⓓ

18. The U.S. clothing manufacturing industry is facing an __________ competitive global market.
(A) increasingly (B) increasing
(C) increase (D) increased
Ⓐ Ⓑ Ⓒ Ⓓ

19. The elevator in the south wing of the building will be shut down for routine __________ for most of the morning on Friday.
(A) to maintain (B) maintaining
(C) maintained (D) maintenance
Ⓐ Ⓑ Ⓒ Ⓓ

20. Though __________ planned for August, the company picnic has been moved up to the last weekend of July.
(A) originality (B) original
(C) originally (D) origins
Ⓐ Ⓑ Ⓒ Ⓓ

Part 6 Text Completion

Read the text that follows. A word, phrase, or sentence is missing in parts of the text. Select the best answer to complete the text.

Questions 21-24 refer to the following article.

Changing the Way People Have Fun in San Bernardino

The opening of the Cinema Sixteen multiplex in San Bernardino features many special offerings in an attempt to attract large audiences. Tickets, normally $11.00 for 2-D films and $15.00 for 3-D screenings, -------
21. discounted by $4.00 for the next one month. This discount is sure to produce sold-out screenings.

Also, Cinema Sixteen will host special all-night events on its first four weekends with horror, science-fiction, romance and adventure film festivals. The manager of Cinema Sixteen explains, "We want people to think of Cinema Sixteen as a special place, with -------
22. events during all seasons of the year. Cinema Sixteen will always be exciting."

Different from other multiplexes, Cinema Sixteen includes a much larger food and drink -------. -------.
23. **24.**

21. (A) have been
(B) were being
(C) will be
(D) will have been

Ⓐ Ⓑ Ⓒ Ⓓ

22. (A) broken
(B) frequent
(C) shocking
(D) closed

Ⓐ Ⓑ Ⓒ Ⓓ

23. (A) selective
(B) select
(C) selector
(D) selection

Ⓐ Ⓑ Ⓒ Ⓓ

24. (A) The food stand serves the chefs' original sandwiches only, but the taste is unusually good.
(B) You can enjoy unusual choices such as light Japanese, Mexican and Chinese meals, besides the regular popcorn, hot dogs and soft drinks.
(C) We often remember the memorable cuisine experiences of our childhood days.
(D) It is natural that multiplexes serve a large selection of tasty food.

Ⓐ Ⓑ Ⓒ Ⓓ

Part 7 Single Passage

Read the following text. Select the best answer for each question.

Questions 25-28 refer to the following signboard notice.

WALNUTWOOD MALL

**** Upcoming Events ****

Let us entertain your kids while you take advantage of our first-rate shopping facilities. These events will take place in the Main Plaza, across from the new gift-wrapping station that will be opening on May 1.

May 15 - Roland's Reptile Roadshow

Kids and adults alike will be enthralled by this fun, interactive show featuring snakes, lizards, alligators and more. Kids will have a chance to meet and play with the reptiles after the show!

May 29 - Spring Children's Party

Featuring a performance by Wally the Walnut, our Mall's famous singing mascot. Also featuring face painting and a puppet show. So much fun that your kids may not want to leave!

Make your trip to Walnutwood Mall an outing with the whole family. And remember: Throughout May, we will also be offering all of our customers half-price parking as well as discount coupons for all of our stores. See you then!

25. What is the purpose of the notice?

(A) To encourage families to shop at the mall
(B) To entertain kids and adults by playing with animals
(C) To offer patrons discount coupons
(D) To invite children to a Spring Party

Ⓐ Ⓑ Ⓒ Ⓓ

26. What will open on May 1?

(A) Walnutwood Mall
(B) The Main Plaza
(C) The gift-wrapping station
(D) The parking lot

Ⓐ Ⓑ Ⓒ Ⓓ

27. What can visitors do on May 15?

(A) Watch a musical performance
(B) Play with puppets
(C) Enjoy a wildlife show
(D) Have their faces painted

Ⓐ Ⓑ Ⓒ Ⓓ

28. What is NOT being offered at Walnutwood Mall in May?

(A) Store coupons
(B) Events for children
(C) Gift-wrapping service
(D) Free parking

Ⓐ Ⓑ Ⓒ Ⓓ

Unit 4 Meetings

Warm-up

Vocabulary

空欄に下から適切な語句を選んで書き入れなさい。なお、動詞については原形で記されています。必要に応じて適切な形に変えなさい。

1. Please check the agenda of the next meeting on the (   ) board.
2. One of our clients often (   ) our office and asks the manager lots of questions.
3. The sales (   ) of KNS Inc. discussed effective sales strategies.
4. John Wilkins will (   ) a panel discussion this afternoon at the seminar.
5. The board of (   ) of ABS Motors discussed the company's safety standards this weekend.
6. The personnel department is in charge of selecting well-qualified (   ) for the company.

drop in	chair	directors
employees	bulletin	representatives

TOEIC® Listening

Part 1 Photographs

14

You will hear four short statements. Look at the picture and choose the statement that best describes what you see in the picture.

1.

Ⓐ Ⓑ Ⓒ Ⓓ

2.

Ⓐ Ⓑ Ⓒ Ⓓ

You will hear a question or statement and three responses. Listen carefully, and choose the best response to the question or statement.

3. Mark your answer on your answer sheet. (A) (B) (C)

4. Mark your answer on your answer sheet. (A) (B) (C)

5. Mark your answer on your answer sheet. (A) (B) (C)

6. Mark your answer on your answer sheet. (A) (B) (C)

You will hear a short conversation between two or more people. Listen carefully, and select the best response to each question.

7. What is the woman's problem?
(A) Her smartphone is broken.
(B) She cannot reach Stacy.
(C) She cannot meet Stacy's supervisor.
(D) Her co-worker cannot assist her. (A) (B) (C) (D)

8. What does the man say about Stacy?
(A) She cannot check the woman's message right now.
(B) She is going to meet his supervisor.
(C) She fixed his smartphone.
(D) She uses her laptop for video conferences. (A) (B) (C) (D)

9. What does the man suggest the woman do?
(A) Wait for Stacy's reply
(B) Meet Stacy in person
(C) Go to Stacy's house
(D) Meet the man's boss instead (A) (B) (C) (D)

You will hear a short talk given by a single speaker. Listen carefully, and select the best response to each question.

10. What happened to the woman?
(A) She met with a traffic accident.
(B) Her flight schedule has been changed.
(C) She cannot attend the meeting.
(D) She cannot be a presenter today.
Ⓐ Ⓑ Ⓒ Ⓓ

11. What does the woman ask the man to do?
(A) Change the order of today's presentations
(B) Give a presentation after Jim Wilson
(C) Announce to everyone that the meeting is cancelled
(D) Ask everyone for a favor
Ⓐ Ⓑ Ⓒ Ⓓ

12. What will the woman do for the man in return?
(A) Chair the meeting
(B) Prepare the agenda for the next meeting
(C) Book an airline ticket tomorrow
(D) Buy him lunch tomorrow
Ⓐ Ⓑ Ⓒ Ⓓ

Useful Expression

I'm free from 2:00 to 4:00.

このfreeは「暇な、用事が入っていない」という意味です。よって上の文は「2時から4時の間なら空いていますよ」という意味になります。

A: I'd like to talk about a new marketing plan with you. Would you spare some time for me?
（新しいマーケティングプランについてお話させていただきたいのですが、お時間を取っていただけないでしょうか。）

B: Sure. I'm free from 2:00 to 4:00, so please come to my office any time you like around that time.
（もちろんいいですよ。2時から4時までは空いていますので、そのころいつでもご都合のよろしいときに私のオフィスまで来てください。）

"What do you do in your free time?"（暇なときは何をしていますか）など、freeは会話でもよく使われますので、覚えておきましょう。

Grammar

分詞

<例題> 次の空所に当てはまる語句を記号で選びなさい。

① You have to submit ___________ documents to apply for the grant.
(A) write (B) writing (C) written (D) to write

② People ___________ to take paid leave for the next week can do so.
(A) wish (B) wishing (C) wished (D) to wish

分詞はもともと動詞から派生しており動詞の性質を持っていますが、形容詞や副詞としての働きもします。現在分詞（-ing形）と過去分詞（-ed形）がありますが、どちらを選ぶべきか迷ってしまうことがあるかもしれません。

ポイントは、修飾しているもの（例えば名詞）と分詞との関係です。修飾しているもの（名詞）が分詞で示そうとしている動作を「起こしている」ときには現在分詞（-ing形）が用いられます。それに対して、修飾しているもの（名詞）が分詞で示す動作を「受け取る」場合は過去分詞（-ed形）が用いられます。

例題 ① の分詞は名詞documentを前から修飾しています。documentとwriteの関係ですが、documentは文書であることから「物」であり、物が「書く」ことはできません。文書は「書かれる」もので、The document was written ... のように**writeは受動態の形になります**。このことから、過去分詞である-ed形の (C) writtenが答えになります。

例題 ② の分詞は名詞peopleを後ろから修飾しています。人々（people）がto take... 以下の内容を願うという動作を起こすことができ、People wish [are wishing] to... のように、**wishは能動態の形になります**。よって、現在分詞である-ing形の (B) wishingが答えになります。言い換えれば、分詞が修飾している名詞句が、分詞で始まる部分の主語になっていると言えます。

以上のことから、現在分詞（-ing形）を選ぶか過去分詞（-ed形）を選ぶかについては、**分詞が修飾している名詞句と、分詞の部分との関係を考えるとよい**ということになります。
分詞はいつも名詞を修飾するとは限りません。以下のような形もあります。

<例文> (i) The baby kept **crying** all night long.（その赤ん坊は一晩中泣き続けていた。）
(ii) About 40 percent of voters still remain **undecided** about who they'll vote for.（約40パーセントの有権者が誰に投票するかまだ決めずにいます。）

keepやremainだけでは意味が完結しないため（＝不完全自動詞）、後に分詞を置き、分詞は補語として働きます。例文 (i) では、cryと主語the babyを用いた文は、The baby was crying. のように、能動態の形となります（赤ん坊が「泣く（cry）」という動作を起こしています）。よって、-ing形のcryingをkeepの後に置きます。

例文 (ii) は少し注意が必要です。Voters are undecided. のように、be undecidedの形を作って、「決めていない」の意味になります。つまりundecidedは形容詞的な働きをします。このことから、remainの後に置かれる語は、分詞形容詞の形であるundecidedになります。このように動詞の後に置かれる「分詞」は、動詞（keep, remain）が絡んでいることから、動詞との関わりを考える必要があり、例題で述べた名詞との関係に加えて、分詞で出てくる語が分詞を用いた形容詞としてどのような形で使われるかを考える必要があります。

（例題解答・訳）
① C（その助成金に申し込むには、記入した書類を提出する必要があります。）
② B（来週有給休暇を取りたい人たちは、取ることができます。）

TOEIC® Reading

Part 5 Incomplete Sentences

A word or phrase is missing in each of the sentences below. Select the best answer to complete the sentence.

13. The man ________ in the front row was sleeping, so there is no way that he would ever remember the contents of this wonderful movie.

(A) sits (B) sat
(C) sitting (D) being sat

Ⓐ Ⓑ Ⓒ Ⓓ

14. The noise ________ from the construction site made it difficult for the staff to concentrate on their tasks.

(A) producing (B) produce
(C) productions (D) produced

Ⓐ Ⓑ Ⓒ Ⓓ

15. All things ________, his numerous complaints about your work could be caused by his jealousy.

(A) consider (B) considered
(C) considering (D) consideration

Ⓐ Ⓑ Ⓒ Ⓓ

16. For further information ________ this medication, please call the K&M Pharmacy customer service department.

(A) concerns (B) concerning
(C) concern (D) concerned

Ⓐ Ⓑ Ⓒ Ⓓ

17. Next month's article will cover the actress who was ________ in last year's most successful production.

(A) featured (B) a feature
(C) to feature (D) featuring

Ⓐ Ⓑ Ⓒ Ⓓ

18. With its unusual taste of Chinese cuisines, Bei-Wei Restaurant offers a ________ dining experience in the town.

(A) surprise (B) surprisingly
(C) surprising (D) surprised

Ⓐ Ⓑ Ⓒ Ⓓ

19. The trouble is that our suppliers are unable to provide ________ materials to complete construction.

(A) of remaining (B) our remaining
(C) remained (D) the remaining

Ⓐ Ⓑ Ⓒ Ⓓ

20. As ________ in last week's meeting, a variety of policy changes will be put into effect from next week.

(A) discuss (B) discussing
(C) discussed (D) discussion

Ⓐ Ⓑ Ⓒ Ⓓ

Part 6 Text Completion

Read the text that follows. A word, phrase, or sentence is missing in parts of the text. Select the best answer to complete the text.

Questions 21-24 refer to the following announcement.

> The annual shareowners' meeting of Continental Shipping Inc. will take place on March 27 at 11:00 in Wadsworth Auditorium of Linder College, 2744 Peachtree Avenue, Atlanta. The decision by the board of directors to _______ (**21.**) World Air Freight will be discussed. The addition of World Air Freight now makes Continental more heavily invested in air transport than in the original business, sea cargo. The board plans to transform the company into an overall freight business _______ (**22.**) discussed. The next step will be the addition of a freight rail system within the next two years.
>
> At the end of their terms of service, three of the 22 members of the board of directors are going to retire from the company and the vacancies need to be filled. To select the board of directors by vote, please use the enclosed ballot _______ (**23.**) drop it into the ballot box.
>
> Under business regulations, a board election with fewer than 50 percent of the sharers voting is invalid. _______ (**24.**). This is a significant expense, so be sure you vote your shares by following the option described above.

21. (A) require
(B) acquaint
(C) refine
(D) acquire

Ⓐ Ⓑ Ⓒ Ⓓ

22. (A) will be
(B) was
(C) is being
(D) has been

Ⓐ Ⓑ Ⓒ Ⓓ

23. (A) as
(B) or
(C) and
(D) but

Ⓐ Ⓑ Ⓒ Ⓓ

24. (A) In this case, voting must be held again.
(B) According to the regulations, voting must be done by shareholders.
(C) Electronic voting is still too early to implement.
(D) Candidates running for office must meet certain qualifications.

Ⓐ Ⓑ Ⓒ Ⓓ

Read the following text. Select the best answer for each question.

Questions 25-28 refer to the following announcement.

JULY CONFERENCE ANNOUNCEMENT

Saturday, July 6, 2024

4:30 pm – 5:30 pm - Robbie Keane, Presentation: "Staff Management"

Robbie Keane of the Personnel Department will be presenting training programs for new employees.

5:30 pm – 6:30 pm - Panel Discussion

Experts from several leading companies will discuss employee training and answer questions from the audience.

6:30 pm – 7:30 pm - Fellowship Hour, Dinner

PLACE: The Hummer Tower, 3220 Bianca Road
COST: $18 for members / $25 for non-members
RESERVATIONS: Please contact Costas Antonakis
at Tel 386-638-3511, ext. 240 / Fax 386-638-7501.

25. What is the topic for the conference?

(A) Annual budget

(B) Personnel matters

(C) Financial matters

(D) Maintenance fee

Ⓐ Ⓑ Ⓒ Ⓓ

26. How much does a non-member need to pay for the conference?

(A) $3

(B) $17

(C) $18

(D) $25

Ⓐ Ⓑ Ⓒ Ⓓ

27. How long does the event last?

(A) One hour

(B) Two hours

(C) Three hours

(D) All day

Ⓐ Ⓑ Ⓒ Ⓓ

28. What is NOT true about the conference?

(A) It will be held at the Hummer Tower.

(B) There will be a question-and-answer session.

(C) People have to send e-mail for reservations.

(D) Robbie Keane will make a presentation.

Ⓐ Ⓑ Ⓒ Ⓓ

Unit 5 Personnel

Warm-up

Vocabulary

空欄に下から適切な語句を選んで書き入れなさい。なお、動詞については原形で記されています。必要に応じて適切な形に変えなさい。

1. I saw a job advertisement this morning and checked the salary for the ( ).
2. The president of Cat Computer resigns this week and Terry Marx ( ) the position.
3. The plant manager is in charge of ( ) the workers and protecting their security.
4. New employees should check the details of the ( ) before they sign it.
5. Please send your ( ) to the manager by the end of this month, if you plan to apply for the internship position.
6. The company decided to ( ) three qualified candidates.

position	supervise	résumé
contract	hire	take over

TOEIC® Listening

Part 1 Photographs

18

You will hear four short statements. Look at the picture and choose the statement that best describes what you see in the picture.

1.

Ⓐ Ⓑ Ⓒ Ⓓ

2.

Ⓐ Ⓑ Ⓒ Ⓓ

Part 2 Question-Response 19

You will hear a question or statement and three responses. Listen carefully, and choose the best response to the question or statement.

3. Mark your answer on your answer sheet. Ⓐ Ⓑ Ⓒ

4. Mark your answer on your answer sheet. Ⓐ Ⓑ Ⓒ

5. Mark your answer on your answer sheet. Ⓐ Ⓑ Ⓒ

6. Mark your answer on your answer sheet. Ⓐ Ⓑ Ⓒ

20

You will hear a short conversation between two or more people. Listen carefully, and select the best response to each question.

7. What has happened to the man?
(A) He has decided to leave the company.
(B) He has been offered a promotion.
(C) He has requested a new assistant.
(D) He has just started his career. Ⓐ Ⓑ Ⓒ Ⓓ

8. What happened last month?
(A) The Oahu Mall store opened.
(B) Robert got a new job.
(C) Robert moved to a different store.
(D) The store manager quit. Ⓐ Ⓑ Ⓒ Ⓓ

9. What will the current Oahu manager do?
(A) Work under Robert
(B) Stay where he is
(C) Find a new job
(D) Quit the company Ⓐ Ⓑ Ⓒ Ⓓ

Part 4 Talk 21

You will hear a short talk given by a single speaker. Listen carefully, and select the best response to each question.

10. How many years of management experience are necessary?

(A) Two
(B) Three
(C) Four
(D) Five

11. What is a job responsibility of the position?

(A) Editing textbooks
(B) Ordering books
(C) Teaching courses
(D) Recruiting new staff

12. What are applicants asked to do?

(A) Take a written test
(B) Call the administration office
(C) Go to the bookstore
(D) Submit their résumés

Useful Expression

I'm getting used to it.

「(それに) 慣れてきました」という言い方です。get used toは「～に慣れる」という意味で、現在進行形で言うことにより「だんだんと慣れてきている」という意味を示します。

A: How about your new job? You started a new career, so I think you have to learn lots of things.
(新しい仕事はどうだい。新しい職種なので、覚えなければならないことが多いと思うけど。)

B: I'm getting used to it. Since I had no experience with my new job, I have much to learn now. But I receive job instructions from my boss and have the support of my colleagues. So I'm happy with this change.
(慣れてきたよ。新しく始めた仕事については全く経験がなかったので今いろいろ覚えなければならないけど、上司から指導を受けているし、同僚の支えもあるので、仕事を変えてよかったと思っているよ。)

現在進行形で言うことにより、だんだんと慣れてきている様子がよく伝わりますね。

Grammar

不定詞と動名詞 (1)

＜例文＞ (i) ○ I promise to come here tomorrow.
× I promise coming here tomorrow.
(ii) × I gave up to study German.
○ I gave up studying German.

動詞によって (i) のように目的語に不定詞しか取ることができないものもあれば、(ii) のように動名詞しか取ることができないものもあります。動詞が不定詞と動名詞のどちらを取るのか、見分ける術はあるのでしょうか。

不定詞のみを取るもの、動名詞のみを取るもの、それぞれ代表的な動詞を挙げてみましょう。

【不定詞のみを取る動詞】
aim, decide, desire, expect, hope, promise, refuse, want, wish など

【動名詞のみを取る動詞(句)】
avoid, enjoy, escape, finish, give up, mind, practice, put off, quit など

不定詞のみを取る動詞は、時間的に「未来」のことや「先」のことに関係するものが多いことが分かります。それに対して、動名詞はそのような傾向はないことが分かります。つまり、不定詞は未来指向であると言えます。例文 (i) の promiseの場合、これから行うことについて約束するわけですから、未来指向のto不定詞と結びつきやすいというわけです。

このことから、不定詞と動名詞どちらも取る動詞であっても、中には意味が異なる場合もあることが分かってきます。rememberを例に考えてみましょう。

(iii) Please remember to enclose a self-addressed, stamped envelope.
(住所を書いて切手を貼った封筒を同封するのを忘れないでください。)

(iv) I don't remember studying physics in my undergraduate days at all.
(大学の学部時代に物理学を学んだことは全く思い出せません。)

(iii) の場合はrememberはto不定詞と結びついており、「これから先に行うこと」を示すため、これからすることを「覚えておく」という意味になります。(iv) の場合はrememberは動名詞と結びついており、未来のことではなくこれまでのことに焦点が当たった「思い出す」という意味になります。

英文にたくさん触れて、このような不定詞と動名詞の違いを認識できるようになりましょう。

TOEIC® Reading

Part 5 Incomplete Sentences

A word or phrase is missing in each of the sentences below. Select the best answer to complete the sentence.

13. I remember __________ to Jeff Crystal at the high school commencement 10 years ago, but I can't recall his face.

(A) to talk (B) talks
(C) talking (D) talked

Ⓐ Ⓑ Ⓒ Ⓓ

14. Mr. Dell refrained from __________ any comment because he believed he had nothing to be blamed for.

(A) making (B) to make
(C) made (D) being made

Ⓐ Ⓑ Ⓒ Ⓓ

15. Claudia wants to be a flight attendant of an international airline, so it has become a part of her routine to imagine herself __________ by air.

(A) traveling (B) to travel
(C) traveled (D) being traveled

Ⓐ Ⓑ Ⓒ Ⓓ

16. We have just finished writing our proposal for a new project and the last thing we have to do is to have Tim __________ our English on it.

(A) checking (B) to check
(C) checked (D) check

Ⓐ Ⓑ Ⓒ Ⓓ

17. It is no good __________ Ted to lend you money; he's very stingy with his money.

(A) to ask (B) asking
(C) ask (D) asked

Ⓐ Ⓑ Ⓒ Ⓓ

18. After her hard work in recent months, Ms. McClowsky has finally found out where __________ the computer parts.

(A) order (B) will order
(C) to order (D) ordering

Ⓐ Ⓑ Ⓒ Ⓓ

19. It's worth __________ that the updating of the security software on this computer is free to use for only one time.

(A) to remember (B) remembering
(C) remembered (D) remember

Ⓐ Ⓑ Ⓒ Ⓓ

20. When entering the plant premises, all vehicles are subject to __________ for security reasons.

(A) inspect (B) be inspected
(C) inspecting (D) inspection

Ⓐ Ⓑ Ⓒ Ⓓ

Part 6 Text Completion

Read the text that follows. A word, phrase, or sentence is missing in parts of the text. Select the best answer to complete the text.

Questions 21-24 refer to the following article.

Orientation for New Employees

Employee orientation ensures that new employees understand the policies and procedures of a business organization. It helps employees understand how their jobs fit into the company's operations. It also covers personnel procedures, from _______ (**21.**) the contract of employment to banking and tax details that will ensure they get paid without hesitation.

FR Morgan Inc. considers employee orientation to be a key training activity. Over the years, the company's orientation has evolved into a week-long program. ________ (**22.**). On other days, the employees learn about how the company operates. They also learn communication techniques and how to perform _______ (**23.**) functions in the company. By the review session on the last day, the employees are ready to start work. In addition, they are prepared to deliver the highest level of customer service.

The company believes that its orientation program has helped it to retain its employees. Employees who understand how the company works as _______ (**24.**) as how to perform their job properly are more likely to stay for a long time.

21. (A) leaving
(B) advancing
(C) declining
(D) signing

Ⓐ Ⓑ Ⓒ Ⓓ

22. (A) The company will provide accommodation, so participants do not need to book hotels by themselves.
(B) For one day, managers talk to new employees
about the philosophy of the company.
(C) The orientation program is designed for all the employees to review the history of the company.
(D) With a solid orientation program, the executives can build a strong relationships with the new employees.

Ⓐ Ⓑ Ⓒ Ⓓ

23. (A) variety
(B) various
(C) variously
(D) vary

Ⓐ Ⓑ Ⓒ Ⓓ

24. (A) long
(B) much
(C) soon
(D) well

Ⓐ Ⓑ Ⓒ Ⓓ

Read the following text. Select the best answer for each question.

Questions 25-28 refer to the following job advertisement.

Royal Prince Cruises now offering exciting career opportunities

Working for **Royal Prince Cruises** is ideal if you are looking for some adventure and enjoy working in a challenging and unique environment. We employ individuals from over 60 countries, and we welcome you to join our talented and diverse team! We are looking for servers in our cafeterias, as well as a public relations officer and a navigation officer. Applicants must be at least 18 years of age or older.

Here at **Royal Prince Cruises**, we understand how challenging it can be for our crew to work away from home for such long periods of time. Therefore, as a company we do our best to help give you all the necessary resources and comforts to enable you to be the best host you can be for our guests.

While working onboard a **Royal Prince** cruise ship, you can enjoy:
• Furnished living accommodations
• Crew cafeterias
• Laundry facilities and services
• Crew shops (with discounted convenience items such as toiletries and snacks)

To apply, send an e-mail with a résumé and cover letter stating your preferred position to Merrill Stubing at: jobs@royal-prince-cruises.com

25. According to the job advertisement, why might working at Royal Prince Cruises be difficult?

(A) Staff must do so many tasks on board.
(B) Staff must offer services in many languages.
(C) Staff must handle many guests' needs.
(D) Staff must be away from home for long periods of time. Ⓐ Ⓑ Ⓒ Ⓓ

26. What are onboard employees of Royal Prince Cruises NOT allowed to use?

(A) The ship captain's cabin
(B) Rooms supplied with furniture
(C) Crew cafeterias
(D) Laundry facilities Ⓐ Ⓑ Ⓒ Ⓓ

27. What information should an applicant include to get a job with Royal Prince Cruises?

(A) How they found out about this recruitment
(B) What kind of job they would like
(C) When they can start working on board
(D) When they would like to have a job interview Ⓐ Ⓑ Ⓒ Ⓓ

28. What should the applicants do to apply for the job?

(A) Contact the firm by phone
(B) Fill out a form on the company's website
(C) E-mail the necessary documents to the office
(D) Come to the cruise ship in person Ⓐ Ⓑ Ⓒ Ⓓ

Unit 6 Shopping

TOEIC®

Warm-up

Vocabulary

空欄に下から適切な語句を選んで書き入れなさい。なお、動詞については原形で記されています。また、選択肢の語句は文頭に来るものも小文字で書かれています。必要に応じて適切な形に変えなさい。

1. Their doughnuts are so popular that people always (   ) at the shop to get some.
2. The owner of ABC Grocery usually (   ) on Wednesdays.
3. Cambridge Pizza (   ) of their tasty pizzas and reasonable prices.
4. (   ) will take place within three days after we receive your order.
5. Since I (   ) to work on the train, I often stop by a department store near the station.
6. The repairman is (   ) a flat tire on my car.

offer a discount	fix	shipment
boast	wait in line	commute

TOEIC® Listening

Part 1 Photographs

22

You will hear four short statements. Look at the picture and choose the statement that best describes what you see in the picture.

1.

Ⓐ Ⓑ Ⓒ Ⓓ

2.

Ⓐ Ⓑ Ⓒ Ⓓ

Part 2 Question-Response 23

You will hear a question or statement and three responses. Listen carefully, and choose the best response to the question or statement.

3. Mark your answer on your answer sheet. Ⓐ Ⓑ Ⓒ

4. Mark your answer on your answer sheet. Ⓐ Ⓑ Ⓒ

5. Mark your answer on your answer sheet. Ⓐ Ⓑ Ⓒ

6. Mark your answer on your answer sheet. Ⓐ Ⓑ Ⓒ

You will hear a short conversation between two or more people. Listen carefully, and select the best response to each question.

7. Who is the woman?

(A) A waitress
(B) A manager
(C) A customer
(D) A cashier

8. Look at the graphic. What is the problem with the coupon?

(A) It applies to products under $20.
(B) It must be approved by the supervisor.
(C) The date has expired.
(D) It is for purchases of more than $100.

Ⓐ Ⓑ Ⓒ Ⓓ

BAHAY'S OUTLET STORE
230 S. Brand Blvd. · (912) 104-1310
DISCOUNT COUPON*
$20.00 off
>>**Code number: 957328**

*Offer applies only to purchases over $100.
Expires December 31.*

9. How will the woman help the man?

(A) She will cancel the order.
(B) She will print another discount coupon.
(C) She will call a store employee to assist the customer.
(D) She will ship the items to the man's address.

25

You will hear a short talk given by a single speaker. Listen carefully, and select the best response to each question.

10. What is indicated about pears?

(A) They are from Australia.
(B) The price is $1.25 each.
(C) They are fresh.
(D) They will be sold out soon.

Ⓐ Ⓑ Ⓒ Ⓓ

11. What is the price of T-bone steaks?

(A) $2　(B) $1.25
(C) $3.59　(D) $3.95

Ⓐ Ⓑ Ⓒ Ⓓ

12. What can you find in Aisle 4?

(A) Soup　(B) Pears
(C) Meat　(D) Cheese

Ⓐ Ⓑ Ⓒ Ⓓ

Useful Expression

I was wondering if...

「〜ではないかと思いますが…」という意味で、質問を切り出すときによく用いられます。if の後には文が続きます。質問は現在行われているので "I am wondering if..." のように現在進行形を使ったり、I wonder if...のように現在形を使ったりもしますが、I was wondering if...のように過去進行形を使うことで、「〜と思っていたのですが…」というニュアンスが出て、丁寧さが生まれます。Can you ...? よりCould you...? を用いることで丁寧さや相手への配慮が生まれますが、それと似ていますね。

A: I was wondering if you might run out of cash with that new project you're working on.
(あなたが取り組んでいるあの新しいプロジェクトでお金を使い果たすのではないかと思っているのですが…。)

B: Thanks for your concern. I'm planning to ask the manager for some additional funding.
(ご心配ありがとうございます。マネージャーに少し追加でお金を出していただくようにお願いしようと考えています。)

また I was wondering if... はこのように質問するときに使うだけでなく、"I was wondering if you could help me." (私を手伝っていただけないかと思っていたのですが) のように相手に依頼するときにも使えます。

Grammar

不定詞と動名詞 (2)

<例文> (i) The goal of teachers is to become facilitators of learning.
(教師の目標は、学習を促す人になることです。)

(ii) There's a lot to see in Kyoto.
(京都には見るところがたくさんあります。)

(iii) I studied very hard to pass the test.
(試験に合格するために一生懸命勉強しました。)

(iv) We are very happy to hear that you finally got the job you wanted.
(あなたがついに望んでいた職を得たと聞いて、とても嬉しいです。)

(v) She'll grow up to be a good doctor.
(彼女はよい医者になるでしょう。)

Unit 5 ではto不定詞と動名詞の違いを確認し、to不定詞については動詞の目的語として働くものを見ましたが、それ以外にもto不定詞には様々な用法があります。例文を見てみましょう。
例文 (i) のto不定詞は名詞的用法で、「～すること」という意味を示し、be動詞の補部として働いています。例文 (ii) のto不定詞は形容詞的用法で、前の名詞を修飾しています。例文 (iii) から例文 (v) のto不定詞は副詞的用法で、例文 (iii) は「～するために」という「目的」を示しており、例文 (iv) は happyという感情が生まれる「原因」を示しています。例文 (v) は「結果」を示す言い方です。

to不定詞を取る動詞の中には、to不定詞の前に「人」を表す名詞を置き、この名詞がto不定詞で示した動作の主体を示している場合もあります。

<例文> (vi) I believe Olivia to be here.
(私はオリビアがここにいると信じています。)

(vii) I want Andrew to hear about this.
(私はアンドリューにこのことについて聞いてもらいたいです。)

(viii) I persuaded Mark to change his mind.
(私はマークに考えを改めるよう説得しました。)

TOEIC® Reading

Part 5 Incomplete Sentences

A word or phrase is missing in each of the sentences below. Select the best answer to complete the sentence.

13. I'm used to __________ in a flat, but someday I'd like to buy a house even if it would take more time to commute.

(A) living (B) live
(C) being lived (D) be lived

14. My grandmother often boasted that she hardly ever got colds, and she eventually lived __________ 100.

(A) be (B) to be
(C) being (D) to being

Ⓐ Ⓑ Ⓒ Ⓓ

15. It is not good for a sales representative __________ clients his ignorance of the products he sells.

(A) show (B) showing
(C) shows (D) to show

Ⓐ Ⓑ Ⓒ Ⓓ

16. The most common problems __________ businesses in foreign countries will be discussed by the panel of speakers.

(A) facing (B) to face
(C) are facing (D) having been faced

Ⓐ Ⓑ Ⓒ Ⓓ

17. Everyone says that Nathan's essays grab readers' hearts, but I think he cannot be a good writer __________ such errors.

(A) make (B) being made
(C) to make (D) making

Ⓐ Ⓑ Ⓒ Ⓓ

18. They were arrested on a charge of conspiracy to make many people __________ the contracts of purchase of expensive items against their will.

(A) sign (B) signed
(C) signing (D) to sign

Ⓐ Ⓑ Ⓒ Ⓓ

19. Mr. May strongly objected to __________ for parking, claiming that he parked there for just 10 minutes to buy a newspaper.

(A) be charged (B) being charged
(C) have been charged (D) charging

Ⓐ Ⓑ Ⓒ Ⓓ

20. Yesterday, Harold found an interesting book __________ at the bookshop in his neighborhood.

(A) reading (B) read
(C) to read (D) to being read

Ⓐ Ⓑ Ⓒ Ⓓ

Part 6 Text Completion

Read the text that follows. A word, phrase, or sentence is missing in parts of the text. Select the best answer to complete the text.

Questions 21-24 refer to the following advertisement.

Save More at Savings-Plus

Shopping at Savings-Plus is cheaper! With the largest number of supermarkets in the Great Plains area, your family saves more by shopping at Savings-Plus. Savings-Plus buys in larger quantities than the smaller chains and we pass the savings on to you with the best selections and the best prices. We know you see far more _______ (**21.**) deliveries being made at each Savings-Plus store than at our competitors.

Therefore, Savings-Plus food is _______ (**22.**) it can be! _______ (**23.**). Buy non-prescription drugs at our stores, and you'll be sure to take home the best bargains.

Shoppers throughout the region flock to Savings-Plus for all their grocery and pharmacy needs. Our competitors may operate DVD rentals or provide dry cleaning services, and that's fine with us. We'll _______ (**24.**) them earn money in those areas.

But when it comes to your kitchen and bathroom needs, you know you'll find values and unparalleled quality at all of our Savings-Plus stores.

21. (A) frequently
(B) frequency
(C) frequents
(D) frequent

Ⓐ Ⓑ Ⓒ Ⓓ

22. (A) as fresh as
(B) so fresh that
(C) fresher than
(D) more than fresh

Ⓐ Ⓑ Ⓒ Ⓓ

23. (A) Take advantage of the savings, and shop online now.
(B) Those who'd like to get something to eat should visit Savings-Plus.
(C) And the savings don't stop in the grocery section.
(D) Discount coupons are offered only on select days and times.

Ⓐ Ⓑ Ⓒ Ⓓ

24. (A) have
(B) get
(C) let
(D) make

Ⓐ Ⓑ Ⓒ Ⓓ

Read the following text. Select the best answer for each question.

Questions 25-26 refer to the following text message chain.

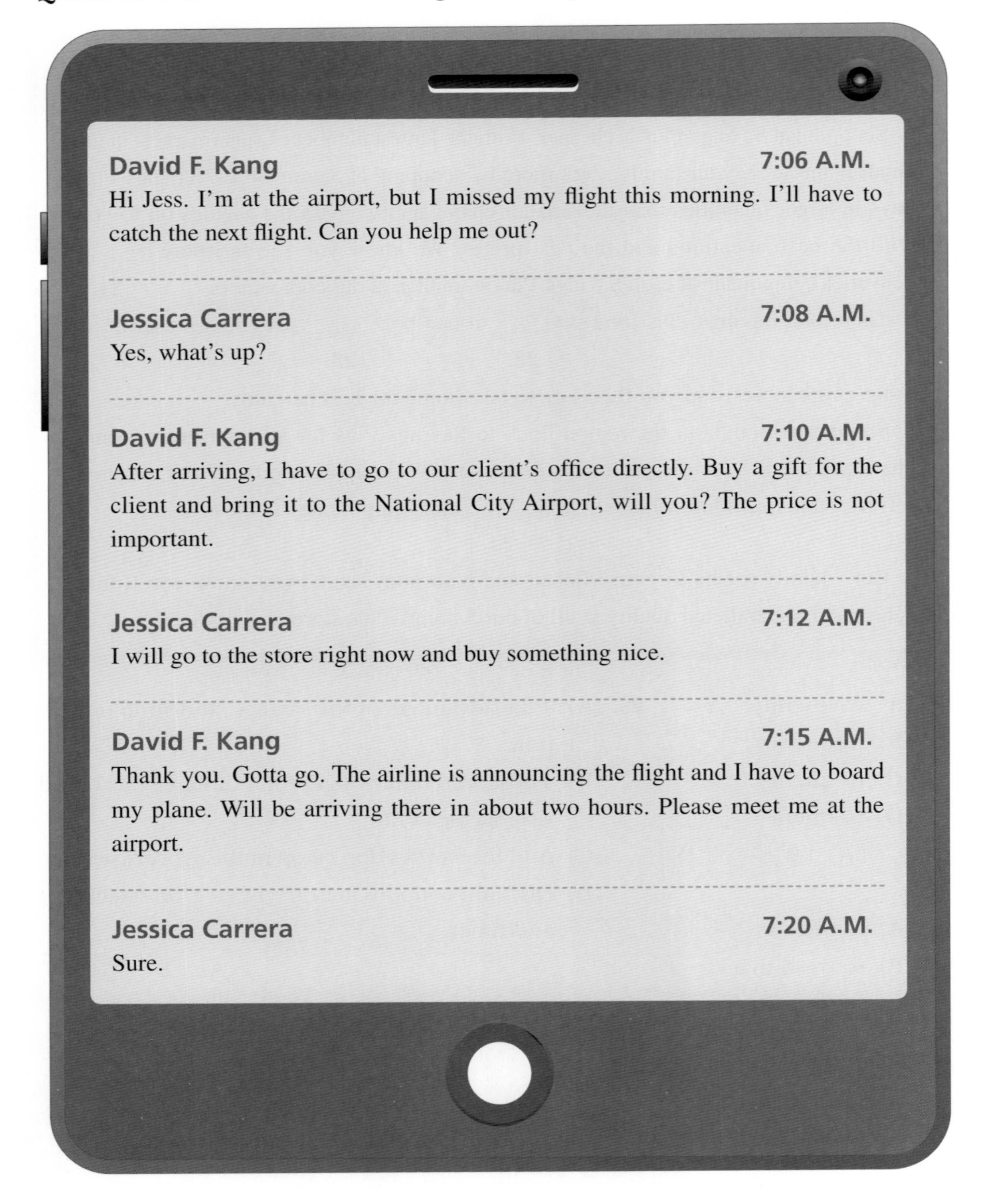

David F. Kang 7:06 A.M.
Hi Jess. I'm at the airport, but I missed my flight this morning. I'll have to catch the next flight. Can you help me out?

Jessica Carrera 7:08 A.M.
Yes, what's up?

David F. Kang 7:10 A.M.
After arriving, I have to go to our client's office directly. Buy a gift for the client and bring it to the National City Airport, will you? The price is not important.

Jessica Carrera 7:12 A.M.
I will go to the store right now and buy something nice.

David F. Kang 7:15 A.M.
Thank you. Gotta go. The airline is announcing the flight and I have to board my plane. Will be arriving there in about two hours. Please meet me at the airport.

Jessica Carrera 7:20 A.M.
Sure.

25. What is suggested about Mr. Kang?

(A) He needs his secretary to buy something.
(B) He is on vacation.
(C) He wants to go to a staff meeting.
(D) He will give a presentation next week.

26. At 7:20 A.M., what does Ms. Carrera mean when she writes "Sure"?

(A) She is happy to talk to Mr. Kang.
(B) She wants to buy a gift.
(C) She thinks Mr. Kang will be late.
(D) She is going to the airport.

Unit 7 Advertisement

Warm-up

Vocabulary

空欄に下から適切な語句を選んで書き入れなさい。なお、動詞については原形で記されています。必要に応じて適切な形に変えなさい。

1. When ( ) a used car, people should check the price on the Internet.
2. Some companies use their own website instead of putting a ( ) in newspapers.
3. The noodle maker gave a ( ) to their customers asking about the image of the company.
4. The poster of the hotel says they offer a ( ) breakfast.
5. Our company decided to ( ) a new project to make environmentally friendly products.
6. The Davis Store ( ) a free brochure that introduces newly published books every Sunday.

issue	classified ad	complimentary
purchase	questionnaire	launch

TOEIC® Listening

Part 1 Photographs

You will hear four short statements. Look at the picture and choose the statement that best describes what you see in the picture.

1.

2.

Ⓐ Ⓑ Ⓒ Ⓓ

Part 2 Question-Response 27

You will hear a question or statement and three responses. Listen carefully, and choose the best response to the question or statement.

3. Mark your answer on your answer sheet. (A) (B) (C)

4. Mark your answer on your answer sheet. (A) (B) (C)

5. Mark your answer on your answer sheet. (A) (B) (C)

6. Mark your answer on your answer sheet. (A) (B) (C)

28

You will hear a short conversation between two or more people. Listen carefully, and select the best response to each question.

7. What is the woman inquiring about?
(A) Submission deadlines
(B) Advertising rates
(C) Size limitations
(D) Topic of the article
(A) (B) (C) (D)

8. When will the next week's issue be published?
(A) Monday
(B) Thursday
(C) Friday
(D) Saturday
(A) (B) (C) (D)

9. What does the man recommend?
(A) Making the ad more colorful
(B) Reducing the size of the article
(C) Submitting the ad early
(D) Giving up the posting
(A) (B) (C) (D)

You will hear a short talk given by a single speaker. Listen carefully, and select the best response to each question.

10. What kind of products does this company sell?

(A) Books and magazines
(B) Hair care products
(C) Posters
(D) Automobiles

11. What is indicated about the romantic design?

(A) It is in black and white.
(B) It is the newest design.
(C) It is not very popular.
(D) It is preferred by women.

12. What does the speaker recommend doing?

(A) Using the design with a romantic couple
(B) Using the design with a single model
(C) Conducting more research
(D) Expanding the market share

Useful Expression

We can't guarantee it.

guaranteeは「保証する、確約する」という意味ですので、上の文は「保証できませんよ」という意味になります。次の文を見てみましょう。

A: I've never seen a whale with my own eyes. I hope I will see one on this whale-watching tour.
(私は直にクジラを見たことがありませんので、このクジラ観察ツアーでクジラに会えるのを楽しみにしているんですよ。)

B: Unfortunately, we can't guarantee it. We'll go to an area far from the shore, so usually we can see some whales there. But since we are passing by a bit later than usual, we are not 100% sure if they will appear this time.
(残念ながら、クジラに会えるのを確約できませんよ。海岸からかなり離れたところに行くのでたいていクジラを見ることができますが、いつもよりちょっと遅いので、今回は100% 必ず出現するとは言えませんね。)

この会話のように、はっきりと約束できないときに使うと効果的な表現です。

Grammar

仮定法

＜例文＞(i) If it rains tomorrow, we'll reschedule the party. ＜直説法＞
（明日雨が降れば、パーティーの日を変更します。）

(ii) If I were rich, I would replace my old computer with a brand-new one.
（お金があれば、古いコンピュータを買い替えて新しいものにするのに。） ＜仮定法＞

英語では、「もし～だったら」と言う場合に、その事柄が現実に起こることかどうかに基づいて言い方を変えます。

例文 (i) は直説法と呼ばれます。if節で示された「明日雨が降る」という事柄は、実際に起こりうるという想定のもと、話をしています。副詞節の中で未来のことを示すときには「現在形」を使いますが、例文 (i) でもif節内の動詞には現在形を用いて、主節は単純に未来を示す助動詞willを用います。

これに対して例文 (ii) は仮定法と呼ばれる言い方です。if節の「私はお金がある」というのは、現実とは異なる事実であり、「仮にそういうことがあった場合...」という仮定のもと、話をしています。if節内の動詞を現在形で言ってしまうと、現在の状況と同じ土俵に立って話をすることになりますので、過去形にして違う流れの話であることを明確にします。少し難しいかもしれませんが、現在形から過去形へと、一つ時制を下げる（前にする）感覚です。なお、be動詞は基本的にwereを用います。また主節にはwould, could, mightといった助動詞を用いて、あくまでも仮定の話であることを示します。

では、過去の事実に対して、事実と異なることを仮定する場合はどうすればよいでしょうか。次の文がそれに当たります。

＜例文＞(iii) If I had realized what you implied in your advice, I wouldn't have messed up at the presentation.
（もし私が君が忠告で示唆していたことに気づいていたら、私は発表で失敗していなかったでしょう。）

if節の中の動詞を過去完了形［had＋過去分詞］にします。これは、過去のことを過去形で言ってしまっては、過去のことと同じ土俵に立つことになりますので、過去完了形にします（こちらも、時制を一つ下げる感覚です）。同じく、主節の述部の部分もwouldn't have messed upのように、助動詞の後を［have＋過去分詞］の形にします。

if節を省略したり、if節とは異なる言い方をする仮定法もあります。以下のものは、その一例です。

＜例文＞

(iv) Should you need any help, you can contact me any time.
（万一助けが必要なら、いつでも私に連絡していただいて構いません。）

(v) Without this translation software, we would have had to hire more interpreters.
（この翻訳ソフトが無ければ、通訳者をもっと多く雇わなければならなかったでしょう。）

(vi) But for her, I couldn't have gotten over my difficulty.
（彼女がいなければ、私は困難から立ち直ることができていなかったでしょう。）

(vii) Bring your ID; otherwise, you couldn't enter the room.
（自分のIDを持って来てください。さもないと、部屋に入ることができないでしょう。）

TOEIC® Reading

Part 5 Incomplete Sentences

A word or phrase is missing in each of the sentences below. Select the best answer to complete the sentence.

13. I'll tell Kate about the details of our business trip if I __________ her tomorrow.
(A) meet (B) will meet
(C) am going to meet (D) will be met
Ⓐ Ⓑ Ⓒ Ⓓ

14. __________ he change his mind, we would never blame him.
(A) If (B) With
(C) Should (D) Unless
Ⓐ Ⓑ Ⓒ Ⓓ

15. __________ we had investigated the merit of our proposal more thoroughly, we wouldn't have failed in the presentation.
(A) If (B) Since
(C) When (D) As
Ⓐ Ⓑ Ⓒ Ⓓ

16. __________ you checked the document in detail, you wouldn't have brought such big damage on your client.
(A) If (B) Had
(C) Should (D) Unless
Ⓐ Ⓑ Ⓒ Ⓓ

17. Some of the staff in the public relations department are demanding that the department chief __________ the company.
(A) leave (B) leaves
(C) will leave (D) left
Ⓐ Ⓑ Ⓒ Ⓓ

18. If Ms. Wong had refused to be transferred to the California office 10 years ago, she __________ the head of the Shanghai office now.
(A) wouldn't be (B) wouldn't have been
(C) won't be (D) will be
Ⓐ Ⓑ Ⓒ Ⓓ

19. Please notice that you must be back here before midnight; __________ you'll be locked out.
(A) if (B) provided
(C) otherwise (D) so that
Ⓐ Ⓑ Ⓒ Ⓓ

20. He __________ not have bought a medium-sized sweater, but it was too late by then.
(A) should (B) would
(C) could (D) might
Ⓐ Ⓑ Ⓒ Ⓓ

Part 6 Text Completion

Read the text that follows. A word, phrase, or sentence is missing in parts of the text. Select the best answer to complete the text.

Questions 21-24 refer to the following memo.

> ***MEMORANDUM***
>
> To: Merkle & Associates Employees
> From: Personnel Department
>
> ---
>
> The personnel department is pleased to announce the upcoming launch of *Around M&A*, a monthly newsletter for and about our organization and its employees. The newsletter _______ (**21.**) to all employees via e-mail on the first Tuesday of each month.
>
> The decision to distribute *Around M&A* electronically was made in order to reduce paper consumption. This is in _______ (**22.**) with our continuing commitment to the conservation of natural resources.
>
> *Around M&A* will feature summaries of organizational _______ (**23.**) as well as news and personal notes about individual employees. _______. (**24.**)

21. (A) distributes
(B) is distributed
(C) has been distributed
(D) will be distributed

Ⓐ Ⓑ Ⓒ Ⓓ

22. (A) contrast
(B) keeping
(C) concern
(D) using

Ⓐ Ⓑ Ⓒ Ⓓ

23. (A) announce
(B) announcing
(C) announcements
(D) announcer

Ⓐ Ⓑ Ⓒ Ⓓ

24. (A) Submissions for inclusion in the periodical can be sent as text documents to: aroundma@merkle.com.
(B) We believe that it's worth waiting for the print version of *Around M&A*.
(C) Nowadays a number of people read a newspaper on their smartphone.
(D) As M&A markets continue to mature, M&A professional lawyers are in high demand nowadays.

Ⓐ Ⓑ Ⓒ Ⓓ

Part 7 Single Passage

Read the following text. Select the best answer for each question.

Questions 25-28 refer to the following advertisement.

CLOSING SALE

After 24 years of service, the Harris Avenue ***HealthCore***® store is closing permanently. Tremendous values are now available for smart shoppers. Hurry — the store will close on March 31, 2024.

Prices apply to the Harris Avenue branch store only. Sorry, once supplies are gone, no rain checks for use at other ***HealthCore***® stores will be issued.

Here are just some of the savings! (A more detailed flyer is available at the store.)

HealthCore® Generic Aspirin, 500 tablets	$4.80 (21% savings)
Clean'N'Soft Rinse, 1 qt. bottle	$3.20 (50% savings)
Freshmint Mouthwash, 1 qt. bottle	$4.50 (38% savings)
Assorted throw rugs, various colors	3 for $8.00 (30% savings)
Kingway Photo Memory Cards, 236-shot size	$19.75 (22% savings)
Sunbuster, sunscreen, 36 SPF	$8.90 (23% savings)
Beach blankets, various patterns	$3.50 (80% savings)

With every purchase of $20 or more, one child per shopper can reach into the surprise bag for a free toy. (Limited to children age 10 or younger)

With a purchase of $40 or more, you can receive a complimentary meal ticket for two at Ranchero Mexicano worth $15, good for the remainder of the year.

We appreciate each and every one of our customers in the community for supporting Harris Avenue ***HealthCore***® for almost a quarter of a century. This is our way of saying: Thank You...and Farewell.

From all of us at Harris Avenue HealthCore®

25. Where can people get these discount prices?

(A) At all HealthCore stores
(B) At Ranchero Mexicano
(C) At some shops on Harris Avenue
(D) At the 24-year-old branch store

Ⓐ Ⓑ Ⓒ Ⓓ

26. Why can people get these discount prices?

(A) The store is closing.
(B) The store has a year-end sale.
(C) The customers need it.
(D) They are good customers.

Ⓐ Ⓑ Ⓒ Ⓓ

27. Which item is reduced the least?

(A) The outdoor blankets
(B) The generic medicine
(C) The floor rugs
(D) The hair-care product

Ⓐ Ⓑ Ⓒ Ⓓ

28. What do people have to do to get the meal ticket offer?

(A) Do some shopping at any HealthCore store
(B) Buy one of the bargains
(C) Make a purchase of $10
(D) Buy $40 or more worth of goods

Ⓐ Ⓑ Ⓒ Ⓓ

Unit 8 Daily Life

Warm-up

Vocabulary

空欄に下から適切な語を選んで書き入れなさい。なお、動詞については原形で記されています。また、選択肢の語句は文頭に来るものも小文字で書かれています。必要に応じて適切な形に変えなさい。

1. The (   ) news says the number of health-conscious teenagers is increasing.
2. If you don't pay your electricity (   ), the electricity might be cut off.
3. You have to send a (   ) for $20 to the school to get their application form.
4. Young children need to have adequate (   ) to grow properly.
5. If you want to open a bank (   ) in foreign countries, you have to show your passport as your identification.
6. (   ) are the photos we took at Billy's wedding ceremony.

check	enclose	account
latest	bill	nutrition

TOEIC® Listening

Part 1 Photographs

You will hear four short statements. Look at the picture and choose the statement that best describes what you see in the picture.

1.

Ⓐ Ⓑ Ⓒ Ⓓ

2.

Ⓐ Ⓑ Ⓒ Ⓓ

Part 2 Question-Response

31

You will hear a question or statement and three responses. Listen carefully, and choose the best response to the question or statement.

3. Mark your answer on your answer sheet. Ⓐ Ⓑ Ⓒ

4. Mark your answer on your answer sheet. Ⓐ Ⓑ Ⓒ

5. Mark your answer on your answer sheet. Ⓐ Ⓑ Ⓒ

6. Mark your answer on your answer sheet. Ⓐ Ⓑ Ⓒ

Part 3 Conversation

32

You will hear a short conversation between two or more people. Listen carefully, and select the best response to each question.

7. Why did Paul call?
(A) To invite Katie to the party
(B) To order a meal
(C) To offer to take food to a party
(D) To cancel a plan Ⓐ Ⓑ Ⓒ Ⓓ

8. What is the woman doing now?
(A) Shopping at the groceries
(B) Buying wine
(C) Setting the table
(D) Cooking pasta Ⓐ Ⓑ Ⓒ Ⓓ

9. What does the woman ask Paul to bring?
(A) A salad
(B) Some cheese
(C) Some wine
(D) Some bread Ⓐ Ⓑ Ⓒ Ⓓ

You will hear a short talk given by a single speaker. Listen carefully, and select the best response to each question.

10. What is the topic of this program?
(A) Party menus
(B) Recipe books around the world
(C) Nutritional balance
(D) Gardening
Ⓐ Ⓑ Ⓒ Ⓓ

11. Which language is the recipe book translated into?
(A) Spanish
(B) Italian
(C) Chinese
(D) English
Ⓐ Ⓑ Ⓒ Ⓓ

12. Why are Lydia's dishes good for little kids?
(A) Lydia uses cheap ingredients.
(B) Lydia uses fewer vegetables in her recipes.
(C) People can cook them quickly.
(D) Most of the ingredients are fresh vegetables and fruits.
Ⓐ Ⓑ Ⓒ Ⓓ

Useful Expression

Would you mind if...?

mindはもともと「～するのをいやがる、気にする」という意味です。よって、上の文は「～するとあなたはいやがりますか／気にしますか」という意味ですが、「～しても／～していただいてもいいでしょうか」というように、何かを依頼するときに用いられます。

気をつけなければならないのは、答え方です。もともとmindは「いやがる、気にする」という意味ですので、聞かれたことについて全く問題ない場合は「気にしませんよ」と答える必要がありますから、Noを意味する言い方を使って答えなければなりません。Yesと言って答えてしまうと、「気にする」ことになり、つまり「了承しません」というように依頼を断ることになってしまうので、注意が必要です。

A: Luke, would you mind if I turn on the stereo and play some music? I'd like to refresh myself.
（ルーク、ステレオで音楽かけてもいいかしら。気分を入れ替えたくって。）

B: Of course not. I feel tired, too. Let's take a break and have some tea.
（もちろんいいよ。ぼくもちょっと疲れてたので、ちょっと休んでお茶でも飲もうか。）

Of course not. の他には、Certainly not. / No, go ahead. / Not at all. のような答え方もあります。

Grammar

受動態

<例題> 次の空所に当てはまる語句を記号で選びなさい。

① The problem ＿＿＿＿＿ by the executives last night.

(A) discussed (B) discussed about
(C) was discussed (D) was discussed about

英語では能動態と受動態をうまく使い分けて、文の中でどこに焦点を当てるか工夫します。TOEIC® L&Rの短文穴埋め問題（Part 5）でも能動態か受動態かを問う問題があり、注意が必要です。大事なことは、問われている動詞が「自動詞」なのか「他動詞」なのかを見分けることです。例文を見てみましょう。

discussはThey discussed the topic.（彼らはその話題について話し合いました。）のように、後に目的語を取る「他動詞」です。例題 ① で (A) のdiscussedを選ぶと、後に続くby the executivesは前置詞byが付いていますので、目的語になりえません。よって、他動詞であるはずのdiscussに目的語がないことになってしまいます。また、(A) discussedを選ぶと、主語のthe problem（その問題）はdiscuss（話し合う）の行為を行う者として解釈することになりますが、the problemは話し合う「対象」であり、そのような解釈はできません。

つまり、例題の文は受動態の形になっており、本来discussの目的語である「対象」を表わすthe problemが主語位置に動いていると考えられます。よって、受動態の形であるbe動詞を伴った (C) was discussed が答えになります。

The executives discussed the problem last night.
⇒The problem **was discussed** ＿＿＿＿＿ by the executives last night.

TOEIC® L&Rの空所補充問題では例題①のような能動態であるのか受動態であるのかを見抜く問題が出ますが、ポイントは動詞が目的語を伴わない「自動詞」であるか、目的語を伴う「他動詞」であるかを理解することです。空所が動詞の形を問う問題の場合、その動詞が他動詞であるのにもかかわらず、空所の後に目的語となる名詞がない場合は、受動態になっていると考えられます。

上では目的語を主語位置に動かす受動態のつくり方を説明しましたが、このように複雑に考えなくても、主語が動詞に対してどういう関係にあるかを考えてもよいでしょう。例題の主語のthe problem（問題）はそれ自身がdiscuss（話し合う）ことはできず、「話し合われる」ものです。よって、be動詞を用いた受動態の形にしなければなりません。

なお、日本語の「～について話し合う」という表現につられて、discussは “discuss about something” の形で用いる自動詞であると勘違いする人が多いので、注意が必要です。英語の感覚と日本語の感覚は同じではありません。

（例題解答・訳）
① C（その問題は昨晩、役員たちによって話し合われました。）

TOEIC® Reading

Part 5 Incomplete Sentences

A word or phrase is missing in each of the sentences below. Select the best answer to complete the sentence.

13. They were __________ to hear that their company would soon merge with their competitor.

(A) confusion (B) confuse
(C) confusing (D) confused
Ⓐ Ⓑ Ⓒ Ⓓ

14. The department store in this area which was __________ over a decade ago will be closed next month.

(A) found (B) founded
(C) finding (D) founding
Ⓐ Ⓑ Ⓒ Ⓓ

15. The new model iPhone will __________ on the market after adding the latest improvements to the former model.

(A) puts (B) have put
(C) put (D) be put
Ⓐ Ⓑ Ⓒ Ⓓ

16. The board of directors is __________the problem of the stock shortage now, as it would damage their business dealings.

(A) discussing (B) discussing about
(C) being discussed (D) being discussed about
Ⓐ Ⓑ Ⓒ Ⓓ

17. Most of the residents in the condominium were __________ the fire that broke out on the second floor last night.

(A) killing by (B) died by
(C) killed in (D) dead in
Ⓐ Ⓑ Ⓒ Ⓓ

18. The production workers were __________ working to meet the September 5 deadline for delivery.

(A) made to keep (B) had keep
(C) let keeping (D) keep
Ⓐ Ⓑ Ⓒ Ⓓ

19. Mr. Fox has been __________ to district manager based on his expertise in the field of financial engineering.

(A) promote (B) promoting
(C) promoted (D) to promote
Ⓐ Ⓑ Ⓒ Ⓓ

20. The clothing company had its design for a fashion show __________ by the former employee.

(A) steal (B) stealing
(C) stolen (D) to steal
Ⓐ Ⓑ Ⓒ Ⓓ

Part 6 Text Completion

Read the text that follows. A word, phrase, or sentence is missing in parts of the text. Select the best answer to complete the text.

Questions 21-24 refer to the following invitation.

You are cordially invited to attend the _______ (**21.**) of Susan Miranda London, daughter of Henry and Veronica London, and Daniel Stephen Presley, son of Edward and Joyce Presley, on the thirteenth day of October at 11:00 a.m.

The ceremony will be held in the main chapel at Third Methodist Church, 5238 S. Johnston Avenue in Westfield. A luncheon reception will _______ (**22.**) follow on the grounds of the home of Susan's grandparents, William and Norma London, at 2890 Sunset Drive, one block from the church. Due to limited parking at the London home, it _______ (**23.**) that guests leave their cars at the church and walk over to the reception. In the event of rain, the reception will be held at the Third Methodist Church social hall. _______. (**24.**)

21. (A) event
(B) union
(C) timing
(D) process

Ⓐ Ⓑ Ⓒ Ⓓ

22. (A) occasionally
(B) partially
(C) immediately
(D) recently

Ⓐ Ⓑ Ⓒ Ⓓ

23. (A) is suggested
(B) suggestive
(C) suggestion
(D) suggestible

Ⓐ Ⓑ Ⓒ Ⓓ

24. (A) I would like to send my congratulation and wish you a very good time.
(B) Your attending our reception has made this day really special and unforgettable.
(C) Your comments would be appreciated.
(D) I would appreciate your reply as soon as possible.

Ⓐ Ⓑ Ⓒ Ⓓ

Read the following text. Select the best answer for each question.

Questions 25-28 refer to the following letter.

Reso Cellular Telecommunications, Inc.
560 Ellis Avenue, Suite 200 • Ottawa, ON M3P 2K5

Ms. Jasmine McReadie
57 Cedar Crescent Hwy.
Nepean, ON M9H 1T1

2 July 2023

Dear Ms. McReadie:

Thank you for the payment of your outstanding Reso Cellular bill for the month of June.

We have now received your check in the amount of $89.72 and restored your telephone service. Therefore, we will charge you an additional $35.00 restoration fee, which will be added to your next month's bill.

In order to prevent this situation from happening again in the future, we recommend that you sign up for our Automatic Deposit Payment (ADP) plan. Under this plan, your monthly bill is paid directly from your bank account or charged to your credit card on the 8th of each month.

Paying by this method saves you the trouble of writing a check each month and ensures that payments are never late or forgotten. To sign up for the ADP plan, please fill out and return the enclosed form.

Thank you for your cooperation. We look forward to serving you in the future.

Connor Quinn

Billing Agent

25. What is the main purpose of this letter?

(A) To suggest the automatic payment plan
(B) To request payment of a bill
(C) To cancel a contract
(D) To report a problem with phone service

Ⓐ Ⓑ Ⓒ Ⓓ

26. What is stated about Ms. McReadie's next bill?

(A) The payment is due on July 2.
(B) The service will not be restored.
(C) The bill will include a restoration fee.
(D) The bill is enclosed with this letter.

Ⓐ Ⓑ Ⓒ Ⓓ

27. How does Ms. McReadie currently pay her Reso Cellular bills?

(A) By personal check
(B) By credit card
(C) By automatic withdrawal
(D) By bank transfer

Ⓐ Ⓑ Ⓒ Ⓓ

28. For what purpose can the enclosed form be used?

(A) To make a monthly payment for May
(B) To renew a contract
(C) To sign up for a new account
(D) To change the method of payment

Ⓐ Ⓑ Ⓒ Ⓓ

Unit 9 Office Work

Warm-up

Vocabulary

空欄に下から適切な語句を選んで書き入れなさい。なお、動詞については原形で記されています。必要に応じて適切な形に変えなさい。

1. If you want to take a day ( ), you have to fill out this form.
2. I called Robert's office this morning, but his assistant said he was not ( ).
3. Our company always invites ( ) guests to celebrate its foundation day.
4. This week, Air-American sells $500 return tickets to Japan ( ).
5. Alfred, in the ( ) department, is leaving next week, so we are planning a farewell party for him for next Friday.
6. This company has decided to ( ) its employees with an opportunity to study abroad for a year.

on a first-come, first-served basis	provide	available
distinguished	accounting	off

TOEIC® Listening

Part 1 Photographs

34

You will hear four short statements. Look at the picture and choose the statement that best describes what you see in the picture.

1.

Ⓐ Ⓑ Ⓒ Ⓓ

2.

Ⓐ Ⓑ Ⓒ Ⓓ

You will hear a question or statement and three responses. Listen carefully, and choose the best response to the question or statement.

3. Mark your answer on your answer sheet. Ⓐ Ⓑ Ⓒ

4. Mark your answer on your answer sheet. Ⓐ Ⓑ Ⓒ

5. Mark your answer on your answer sheet. Ⓐ Ⓑ Ⓒ

6. Mark your answer on your answer sheet. Ⓐ Ⓑ Ⓒ

You will hear a short conversation between two or more people. Listen carefully, and select the best response to each question.

7. What will happen on Friday?
(A) The co-workers will give the man a party.
(B) The co-workers will give Linda a party.
(C) The man will leave the company.
(D) The new schedule will be announced. Ⓐ Ⓑ Ⓒ Ⓓ

8. What will Linda do soon?
(A) Leave the company
(B) Organize an event
(C) Take a day off
(D) Join this company Ⓐ Ⓑ Ⓒ Ⓓ

9. What does the woman suggest the man should do?
(A) Give Linda more work
(B) Put off the party
(C) Quit the job
(D) Change his schedule Ⓐ Ⓑ Ⓒ Ⓓ

You will hear a short talk given by a single speaker. Listen carefully, and select the best response to each question.

10. What is indicated about the new policy?

(A) It will be implemented from next week.
(B) It needs extra expenses.
(C) The policy might not be effective.
(D) The meetings will never be held at the office. Ⓐ Ⓑ Ⓒ Ⓓ

11. How many days a week can the employees work from home under the new policy?

(A) One week
(B) Three weeks
(C) One month
(D) Three days Ⓐ Ⓑ Ⓒ Ⓓ

12. What do the employees need when the new policy starts?

(A) A brand-new desk
(B) Another computer
(C) A video camera
(D) A home studio Ⓐ Ⓑ Ⓒ Ⓓ

Useful Expression

I was planning to take this Friday off.

「今週の金曜日は休みを取るつもりでした」という意味です。この “off” は「休んで」という意味を表します。offにはいろんな意味がありますが、基本的な意味は「離れて」ということです。仕事をしている状態から離れると考えると、「休む」という意味が出てくることが分かりますね。

A: Would you help me arrange a slide show at my presentation this Friday?
(今週の金曜日、私の発表でスクリーンにスライドを映すのを手伝っていただけませんか。)

B: Oh, I was planning to take this Friday off. But if you really need my help, I'll change my holiday plan.
(今週の金曜日は休みを取るつもりだったんですが、もしどうしても助けが必要でしたら、休みの予定を変えますよ。)

Grammar

代名詞

日本語は主語を省略できる言語ですが、英語は省略できません。また英語は同じものを指す場合、同じ名詞を何度も繰り返し使うことを避けます。これらのことから、英語では代名詞がよく用いられます。代名詞で覚えておくべきポイントを押さえておきましょう。

・不定代名詞 another, other, others, the other, the others
どれも「他の」という意味ですが、以下のような違いがあります。

another: 基本的に単数のものを指します。
（例） We're going to have another baby.（私たちにもう一人赤ん坊が生まれます。）

other: 後ろに名詞を伴います。後ろの名詞が単数・複数どちらの場合もあります。
（例） The speakers showed us other examples to explain their plans.
（演説者たちは彼らの計画を説明するために、私たちに他の例を示しました。）

others: 複数の人・ものを指します。後ろに名詞を伴わずに、漠然と「他のもの」を指し示します。
（例） Some use a computer and others use a mobile phone to send e-mails.
（Eメールを送るのに、コンピュータを使う人もいれば、携帯電話を使う人もいます。）

the other: はじめに2つ列挙し、one… the otherの形で用いて、「もう片方は」の意味を表します。
（例） I have two English dictionaries: one is an English-Japanese dictionary and the other is an English-English dictionary.
（私は英語の辞書を2冊持っています。1つは英和辞典で、もう1つは英英辞典です。）

the others:「他のもの全て、残り全て」を意味します。
（例） Some of the books are mine, but the others are my father's.
（本はいくつか私のものですが、残りはみな父のものです。）

TOEIC® Reading

Part 5 Incomplete Sentences

A word or phrase is missing in each of the sentences below. Select the best answer to complete the sentence.

13. Although several employees promised to help, the owner ended up doing most of the work on the project __________.

(A) she (B) her
(C) hers (D) herself

Ⓐ Ⓑ Ⓒ Ⓓ

14. We have contracted Portas Van Lines to transport __________ shipments within the Southwest to reduce costs.

(A) we (B) us
(C) our (D) ourselves

Ⓐ Ⓑ Ⓒ Ⓓ

15. __________ who are interested in volunteer work can attend an information session to learn more about our global efforts for starving children.

(A) That (B) Those
(C) They (D) These

Ⓐ Ⓑ Ⓒ Ⓓ

16. Ms. Ito works at the head office on Monday and Thursday, and she engages in some project work at the Osaka office on __________ days of the week.

(A) another (B) the other
(C) others (D) the others

Ⓐ Ⓑ Ⓒ Ⓓ

17. We did not ask for any additional help from the other staff members of our department because Ms. Givon said that she could tackle the project by __________ .

(A) her (B) herself
(C) it (D) itself

Ⓐ Ⓑ Ⓒ Ⓓ

18. Audience members __________ Wickford students pay $20 each for main-floor seats for rock concerts at Wickford University Hall.

(A) for another (B) the other
(C) another (D) other than

Ⓐ Ⓑ Ⓒ Ⓓ

19. Mr. Bresnan will soon retire, ending __________ distinguished 10-year career as the CEO of the Porter Holdings Corporation.

(A) he (B) his
(C) him (D) himself

Ⓐ Ⓑ Ⓒ Ⓓ

20. We have been recruiting people who have good commands of language, so some of the staff are good at English and __________ are good at Chinese.

(A) another (B) other
(C) others (D) the other

Ⓐ Ⓑ Ⓒ Ⓓ

Part 6 Text Completion

Read the text that follows. A word, phrase, or sentence is missing in parts of the text. Select the best answer to complete the text.

Questions 21-24 refer to the following memo.

TO: All staff
FROM: Stephen Lee
DATE: May 2, 2024
SUBJECT: Network maintenance

Hello everyone,

On Sunday, I _______ (**21.**) routine maintenance work on our network, as well as installing new software. The work will begin at 10:00 A.M. and should take about eight hours to finish. _______ (**22.**). Hence, please do not plan to use your office computer on Sunday.

Before leaving the office on Friday, please be sure to save all the files you are working on and shut down your computer completely. _______ (**23.**) you need to use a computer on Sunday, please see me before the end of this week and I will arrange the use of a laptop for you. Due to the _______ (**24.**) supply, laptops will be available on a first-come, first-served basis.

Have a nice weekend.

Stephen

21. (A) conducted
(B) was to conduct
(C) conduct
(D) will be conducting

Ⓐ Ⓑ Ⓒ Ⓓ

22. (A) During that time, the office network will not be operational.
(B) Computers will be available during the maintenance period.
(C) The president doesn't want to update software installed on office computers.
(D) The company will provide clients with this service for free.

Ⓐ Ⓑ Ⓒ Ⓓ

23. (A) How
(B) Also
(C) If
(D) So

Ⓐ Ⓑ Ⓒ Ⓓ

24. (A) abundant
(B) sufficient
(C) limited
(D) substantial

Ⓐ Ⓑ Ⓒ Ⓓ

Read the following texts. Select the best answer for each question.

Questions 25-29 refer to the following e-mails.

MEMORANDUM

TO: All Staff
FROM: Julia Reyes, Personnel Manager
RE: Feedback on office reorganization plan

It was good to meet you all at last Friday's welcoming luncheon. I am very excited to be working here at Business Enterprise Solutions, and I look forward to getting to know all of you better.

As part of my duties as the new Personnel manager, I will be assessing the efficiency of the office in terms of administrative procedures, staff organization, and the use of physical space.

I would like to obtain your feedback through all stages of this process.

To this end, I will be distributing a questionnaire regarding these issues later today to all departments. I would like you to fill it out and return it to me by next Friday.

I also encourage you to include any comments you may want to share on a separate sheet of paper or in an e-mail to me (jreyes@bes.com).

If you have any other questions, please feel free to contact me or just drop by my office at any time.

To: Julia Reyes <jreyes@bes.com>
From: Ken Stamaker <kstamaker@bes.com>
Date: September 17, 2023
Subject: **IT issues in Accounting Department**

Dear Julia,

Welcome to Business Enterprise Solutions. My name is Ken Stamaker and I am in the accounting department.

I'm sorry I was not able to attend the welcoming luncheon for you last Friday, as I was on an errand at the BES downtown branch. I look forward to meeting you in person at some point in the near future.

I am writing you regarding an IT-related matter that affects office administration procedures a great deal.

The accounting department has been sharing a network printer with the sales team for several months now. This means that confidential printouts can carelessly reach the wrong hands. In fact, just last week, a sales associate accidentally picked up an internal document containing "very sensitive" financial data and nearly faxed it to a client.

As you know, accounting data is supposed to be kept confidential. Thus, I recommend that the accounting department be provided with its own network printer, which no other department will use or have access to.

Thanks for your attention to this matter, Ms. Reyes.

Best regards,
Ken Stamaker

25. What can be understood about Julia Reyes?

(A) She was absent from the luncheon.

(B) She has met Mr. Stamaker before.

(C) She is a new employee.

(D) She will attend a luncheon on Friday.

Ⓐ Ⓑ Ⓒ Ⓓ

26. What is Ms. Reyes asking people to do?

(A) Listen to her feedback

(B) Return to the office

(C) Complete a survey

(D) Attend a meeting

Ⓐ Ⓑ Ⓒ Ⓓ

27. Where was Ken Stamaker last Friday?

(A) At a welcoming luncheon

(B) At a client's office

(C) At the downtown branch

(D) In the IT department

Ⓐ Ⓑ Ⓒ Ⓓ

28. What problem does Mr. Stamaker describe?

(A) A defective fax machine

(B) Errors in an accounting report

(C) Unfair hiring practices

(D) Disclosure of internal data

Ⓐ Ⓑ Ⓒ Ⓓ

29. What does Mr. Stamaker suggest?

(A) That a welcoming luncheon be held

(B) That his department get its own printer

(C) That accounting data be shared with others

(D) That no action needs to be taken

Ⓐ Ⓑ Ⓒ Ⓓ

Unit 10 Business

Warm-up

Vocabulary

空欄に下から適切な語句を選んで書き入れなさい。なお、動詞については原形で記されています。必要に応じて適切な形に変えなさい。

1. The (　　　　　　) from the sales division was turned down.
2. Nick says his father was (　　　　　　) to Oregon as a branch manager last month.
3. Because of the recession, the company has to (　　　　　　) several hundred workers this year.
4. Our company runs a business magazine on a (　　　　　　) budget.
5. The presentation about effective investment was very (　　　　　　) and entertaining.
6. I sent my job (　　　　　　) to the company by e-mail.

application	tight	lay off
transfer	proposal	informative

TOEIC® Listening

Part 1 Photographs

You will hear four short statements. Look at the picture and choose the statement that best describes what you see in the picture.

1.

Ⓐ Ⓑ Ⓒ Ⓓ

2.

Ⓐ Ⓑ Ⓒ Ⓓ

39

You will hear a question or statement and three responses. Listen carefully, and choose the best response to the question or statement.

3. Mark your answer on your answer sheet. Ⓐ Ⓑ Ⓒ

4. Mark your answer on your answer sheet. Ⓐ Ⓑ Ⓒ

5. Mark your answer on your answer sheet. Ⓐ Ⓑ Ⓒ

6. Mark your answer on your answer sheet. Ⓐ Ⓑ Ⓒ

40

You will hear a short conversation between two or more people. Listen carefully, and select the best response to each question.

7. What are they mainly talking about?
(A) Expensive electricity bills
(B) Restructuring of employees
(C) New bonus systems
(D) New personnel manager
Ⓐ Ⓑ Ⓒ Ⓓ

8. Why will the company cut some workers?
(A) To reduce personnel costs
(B) To employ more part-timers
(C) To merge with a larger company
(D) To make more profit
Ⓐ Ⓑ Ⓒ Ⓓ

9. What is NOT included in the woman's suggestions?
(A) Save electricity
(B) Employ part-time workers
(C) Get more bonuses
(D) Review the salary system

You will hear a short talk given by a single speaker. Listen carefully, and select the best response to each question.

10. Who would likely be most interested in this announcement?

(A) Schools
(B) Companies
(C) Sports teams
(D) Investors

11. What is Global Staff.com most proud of?

(A) Staff with good language skills
(B) The number of full-time employees
(C) A big market share
(D) A long history in the business

12. What happened last year?

(A) Their translators became full-time workers.
(B) Their interpreters worked in major firms.
(C) Many people registered with Global Staff.com.
(D) The staff's working conditions have changed.

Useful Expression

Are you kidding?

kidは「冗談を言う、からかう」という動詞です。Are you kidding? は「冗談でしょう、うそでしょう」という意味です。「うそ」を表す英語にlieがありますが、"It's a lie!" とか、"You are telling a lie!" のような言い方はしません。英語のlieには「冗談」の意味はなく、「本当に真実ではないこと」を示しています。よって冗談の意味が含まれている日本語の「うそでしょう」を英語で表現するときはlieを用いずに、kidを用いて、Are you kidding?/ You're kidding. /You must be kidding. のように言わなければなりません。

A: Our boss said that we have to turn in the seminar report by tomorrow morning.
(上司が明日の朝までに、セミナーのレポートを提出するように言っています。)

B: Are you kidding? We just came back from the seminar one hour ago.
(冗談でしょう。1時間前にセミナーから戻ってきたばかりですよ。)

Grammar

数量詞

日本語の感覚と英語の感覚が異なる場合があることを先のコラムで書きましたが、数量詞にも感覚の違いが存在します。例えば、日本語の感覚に引っ張られて(i)のような間違いをする人がいます。

(i) × Almost of the students missed the train.（学生のほとんどが電車に乗り遅れた。）

「almost = ほとんど」と考えて、日本語の「学生のうちのほとんど」という解釈をそのまま英語に当てはめています。almostは副詞ですので、その直後にofを取ることができません。almostを使うならば(ii)のようにallを伴う必要があります。あるいはalmostを用いずに(iii)のようにmostを使うことも可能です。

(ii) ○ Almost all of the students missed the train.
(iii) ○ Most of the students missed the train.

mostについては、気を付けなければならないことがあります。(iii)のmostは名詞で、「～の大多数」ということを示していますが、mostには(iv)のように名詞の前に置いて「たいていの、ほとんどの」の意味を表す形容詞の形もあります。形容詞であることから、(v)のようにmostの後ろに冠詞を伴った名詞を持ってくると間違いとなります。つまり、後ろの名詞が冠詞を伴っているときは(iii)のようにmost ofの形を用い、後ろの名詞が冠詞を伴っていないときは(iv)のようにmostを用います。

(iv) ○ Most students in the class missed the train.
(v) × Most the students in the class missed the train.

日本語の名詞には冠詞が付かないことから、このような違いをつかむのが少し難しいですが、いろんな英文に触れて感覚をつかんでいきましょう。

TOEIC® Reading

Part 5 Incomplete Sentences

A word or phrase is missing in each of the sentences below. Select the best answer to complete the sentence.

13. ________ the employees said that they didn't really want to be transferred to the new branch.

(A) Almost of (B) Most
(C) Most of (D) None

14. The human resources division manager gave his colleagues __________ .

(A) a bit of advices (B) some piece of advices

(C) quite a few advice (D) quite a lot of advice

Ⓐ Ⓑ Ⓒ Ⓓ

15. The marketing department of our company hired __________ graduates with a good academic background.

(A) plenty of (B) the large number of

(C) the great deal of (D) a large amount of

Ⓐ Ⓑ Ⓒ Ⓓ

16. The president encouraged as __________ employees as possible to submit their ideas on the new project.

(A) much (B) every

(C) many (D) none

Ⓐ Ⓑ Ⓒ Ⓓ

17. Most participants at the __________ workshop said that it was interesting and informative.

(A) two days (B) two-day

(C) two-days (D) today

Ⓐ Ⓑ Ⓒ Ⓓ

18. Ms. Kitter practices her French at __________ available opportunity in order to improve her fluency and comprehension.

(A) every (B) many

(C) all (D) both

Ⓐ Ⓑ Ⓒ Ⓓ

19. All applications for the spring term must be submitted __________ later than November 30th in order to be considered.

(A) never (B) till

(C) no (D) none

Ⓐ Ⓑ Ⓒ Ⓓ

20. Since the export of our product has risen sharply, we need __________ in our factory.

(A) some new equipment (B) some new equipments

(C) a new equipment (D) the new equipments

Ⓐ Ⓑ Ⓒ Ⓓ

Part 6 Text Completion

Read the text that follows. A word, phrase, or sentence is missing in parts of the text. Select the best answer to complete the text.

Questions 21-24 refer to the following letter.

Dear Mr. Springer:

Just as you requested in your e-mail of September 25, which came to the MixMax homepage postmaster, I am sending you next year's MixMax spring/summer casual fashion catalogue. The new MixMax casual fashion catalogue _______ many important changes from this year's catalogue.
21.

Please make the wholesale orders for your store based on the new catalogue. _______.
22.

This year, MixMax has added a children's line. With this addition, we can now provide your customers _______ clothes for every generation.
23.

If you have any questions, please feel _______ to call me at (988) 239-0112, ext. 24,
24.
or e-mail me at acallaghan@mixmax.com. I will gladly send you the information you need.

Alan Callaghan
Sales Manager, MixMax

21. (A) produces
(B) includes
(C) requests
(D) classifies

Ⓐ Ⓑ Ⓒ Ⓓ

22. (A) We can accept orders by individuals only.
(B) Now you can request an updated catalogue.
(C) All prices in the catalogue are up to date.
(D) Your comments and criticism are always welcome.

Ⓐ Ⓑ Ⓒ Ⓓ

23. (A) for
(B) by
(C) to
(D) with

Ⓐ Ⓑ Ⓒ Ⓓ

24. (A) free
(B) freely
(C) freedom
(D) freeing

Ⓐ Ⓑ Ⓒ Ⓓ

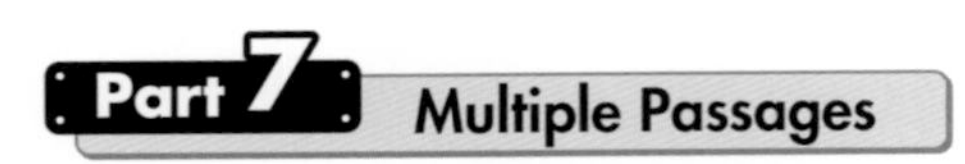

Read the following texts. Select the best answer for each question.

Questions 25-29 refer to the following advertisement and e-mails.

GET A FREE 80-PAGE BOOK:
"10 STEPS TO SUCCESS IN YOUR ESTEEMED CAREER"

Sign up for a one-year subscription to *Modern Entrepreneurs* magazine and get your free book in three easy steps.
1. Buy a copy of *Modern Entrepreneurs*, New York's #1 business magazine.
2. Fill in the application form (on the last page of the magazine).
3. Mail the form and $150 (check or money order) to the address on the last page of the magazine.

TO: Information Desk <info-desk@modern_entrepreneurs.com>
FROM: Linda Borman <lborman@dt-mails.com>
Date: November 1, 2023
Subject: No magazine received

To Whom It May Concern:

I sent my subscription form, mailing address and my e-mail to your company, but I still haven't received my first issue of *Modern Entrepreneurs* magazine yet. I also haven't received the free book. It has been about two months now since I subscribed.

I need the magazine as soon as possible. Can you please let me know when it will be sent? I have to travel to Qatar for a textbook publisher's conference in just two weeks and will certainly need to bring the magazine with me then for networking purposes.

Please respond to my inquiry as soon as possible.

Sincerely,
Linda Borman

TO: Linda Borman <lborman@dt-mails.com>
FROM: Mario Savios <savios-m@modern_entrepreneurs.com>
DATE: November 2, 2023
SUBJECT: Re: No magazine received

Dear Ms. Borman,

Thank you for your e-mail to our Information Desk staff.

Our subscription department staff have checked into the matter, and it looks like we have indeed received your check for $150 and the one-year subscription form. There is no excuse on our part for overlooking this matter, and we are very sorry for the delay.

We will immediately send you the free book copy and your first issue of *Modern Entrepreneurs* magazine by overnight express mail. For your trouble, we will also include a special 25-percent discount coupon that you can use if you decide to renew your subscription next year.

Sincerely,

Mario Savios, Sales Promotion Division
Modern Entrepreneurs Magazine
33 Union Square West
New York, NY 10149

25. What is probably true about the free book?

(A) It is for doctors that work in hospitals.
(B) It is only for successful writers.
(C) It is only for local residents.
(D) It is for everyone who wants to be successful.

A B C D

26. What does Ms. Borman want to do in a couple weeks?

(A) Sign up for a different magazine
(B) Cancel the subscription
(C) Bring the magazine to an overseas conference
(D) Write a thank-you letter

27. In the advertisement, the word "esteemed" in paragraph 1, line 2, is closest in meaning to

(A) happy
(B) amazing
(C) well-known
(D) ordinary

Ⓐ Ⓑ Ⓒ Ⓓ

28. How long will it take for Ms. Borman to receive the book and magazine now?

(A) Another two months
(B) At least two weeks
(C) One more day
(D) An additional year

Ⓐ Ⓑ Ⓒ Ⓓ

29. What reason was given by the company for the delay?

(A) The delivery staff went on strike.
(B) There was no excuse for the oversight.
(C) Daylight savings time caused some confusion.
(D) The payment was not enough.

Ⓐ Ⓑ Ⓒ Ⓓ

Unit 11 Traffic

Warm-up

Vocabulary

空欄に下から適切な語句を選んで書き入れなさい。なお、動詞については原形で記されています。必要に応じて適切な形に変えなさい。

1. The scenic train ride comes to an end, as the train (   ) Paddington Station.
2. Attention (   ) on Flight 395 to Dallas: We're sorry for your inconvenience, but the flight is delayed due to fog.
3. The number of railway accidents has been (   ) over these past two decades.
4. I'll give you a (   ) to the nearest station.
5. All the (   ) parked in this area will be towed away because it is private property.
6. Highway 203 is closed for road construction, and you can get the information on (   ) routes on the website.

alternate	ride	vehicles
decline	passengers	pull into

TOEIC® Listening

Part 1 Photographs

42

You will hear four short statements. Look at the picture and choose the statement that best describes what you see in the picture.

1.

Ⓐ Ⓑ Ⓒ Ⓓ

2.

Ⓐ Ⓑ Ⓒ Ⓓ

Part 2 Question-Response 43

You will hear a question or statement and three responses. Listen carefully, and choose the best response to the question or statement.

3. Mark your answer on your answer sheet. Ⓐ Ⓑ Ⓒ

4. Mark your answer on your answer sheet. Ⓐ Ⓑ Ⓒ

5. Mark your answer on your answer sheet. Ⓐ Ⓑ Ⓒ

6. Mark your answer on your answer sheet. Ⓐ Ⓑ Ⓒ

Part 3 Conversation

44

You will hear a short conversation between two or more people. Listen carefully, and select the best response to each question.

7. Where is this conversation taking place?

(A) At a train station
(B) At a bus stop
(C) At a woman's home
(D) On the bus

Ⓐ Ⓑ Ⓒ Ⓓ

8. What caused the bus to be delayed?

(A) A traffic accident
(B) A workers' strike
(C) Closure of the company
(D) Road construction

Ⓐ Ⓑ Ⓒ Ⓓ

9. What will the man do next?

(A) Ask another passenger's opinion
(B) Check the news on the Internet
(C) Take a taxi instead
(D) Call the bus company

Ⓐ Ⓑ Ⓒ Ⓓ

Part 4 Talk 45

You will hear a short talk given by a single speaker. Listen carefully, and select the best response to each question.

10. Who is this announcement for?

(A) Owners of restaurants
(B) Construction workers
(C) Drivers
(D) Guides

11. What does the traffic information suggest?

(A) Take a different route
(B) Go home early
(C) Get some food
(D) Take Prince Highway

12. What should the listeners do to get more information about the facilities?

(A) Go to the relaxation area
(B) Look at the leaflets
(C) Ask the restaurant staff
(D) Listen to the traffic information

Useful Expression

Don't be so upset.

upsetは「取り乱して、うろたえて、あわてて」という意味です。よって、上の表現は「そんなにあわてないでください」というように、相手を落ち着かせるときに用います。

A: I've just got a phone call from the manager and she says she'll come here in 30 minutes. We should clear the table and put these piles of documents aside.
(たった今マネージャーから電話があって、30分後に来るって言ってるの。テーブルをきれいにして、書類の山を片付けなくっちゃ。)

B: Don't be so upset. I don't think she cares about it. She just wants to see how this office usually goes.
(そんなにあわてないで。マネージャーはそんなこと気にしないと思うわ。いつもオフィスがどんな感じか見たいだけだと思うわ。)

Grammar

接続詞

<例題> 次の空所に当てはまる語句を記号で選びなさい。

① ＿＿＿＿＿ he had a bad headache, he came to the office and gave a presentation.

(A) Though　(B) Despite　(C) In spite of　(D) But

② ＿＿＿＿＿ the fact that she didn't finish her work, she left the office earlier than usual.

(A) Though　(B) Despite　(C) However　(D) If

接続詞は語や句、節をつなぐ働きをします。よくあるのが、本来、節（主語・動詞を伴った文）を取ることができない前置詞を、日本語に引っ張られて接続詞と勘違いしてしまうことです。

例題 ① では、「ひどい頭痛だったにもかかわらず...」という意味になる語を選ぶわけですが、(C) In spite ofは、ofの後に名詞あるいは動名詞を取らなければならないため答えになりえません。このことに気づいた人も、同じ意味を持つ (B) と (C) が選択肢の中にあると、(B) Despiteを接続詞と勘違いして、思わず選んでしまうかもしれません。しかしdespiteは前置詞です。よって後に節（文）を取ることができないため、例題 ① は接続詞である (A) Thoughを選ばなければなりません。

一方、例題 ② の場合は、空所にThoughではなくDespiteを入れなければなりません。

空所に入る語は後に「節」（文）を取っているのではなく、同格節がついた「名詞」を取っています。よって接続詞Thoughではなく、前置詞である (B) Despite（あるいはIn spite of）を選ぶ必要があります。

同じく接続詞と前置詞の違いに関して、接続詞whileと前置詞duringの違いも重要です。両者の違いはTOEIC® L&Rによく出ます。

<例文>

(i) During my first internship experience, I gained immeasurable knowledge and skills.
（私は最初のインターシップの経験で、計り知れないほどの知識と技術を得ました。）

(ii) While working full-time, I studied for my master's in an evening graduate course.
（正社員として働きながら、私は夜間の大学院コースで修士号に向けて勉強しました。）

例文 (i) のduringは「～の間」の意味の前置詞で、those five yearsのような時間の表現や、例文のような一定の時間を示した名詞句を後に取ります。一方、例文 (ii) のwhileは接続詞で、後に節（文）を取ります。例文 (ii) のworkingは動詞由来の「分詞」です（Unit 4文法コラム参照）。文頭にworkingの分詞の形を置いて文と文をつなぐ役割をする、いわゆる「分詞構文」で、例文 (ii) は分詞の前に接続詞も伴っています。あるいは、単にwhileの後にI wasが省略されていると考えても構いません。いずれにしても、後には（分詞、あるいはI wasの省略の形で）文が続いていることになりますので、接続詞whileが用いられます。

（例題解答・訳）

① A（彼はひどい頭痛だったにもかかわらず、会社に来て、発表も行いました。）

② B（彼女は自分の仕事を終えていなかったにもかかわらず、いつもより早めに会社を出ました。）

TOEIC® Reading

Part 5 Incomplete Sentences

A word or phrase is missing in each of the sentences below. Select the best answer to complete the sentence.

13. __________ the time of his presidency, Professor Marc doubled the budget for the research project on DNA in the medical department of the university.

(A) During (B) While
(C) As (D) On

Ⓐ Ⓑ Ⓒ Ⓓ

14. Mr. Tanaka enjoyed his vacation on the island __________ the bad weather he experienced.

(A) regardless (B) despite
(C) although (D) even

Ⓐ Ⓑ Ⓒ Ⓓ

15. Ms. Parker accepted responsibility for neither the incorrect order __________ the mistake in the customer information.

(A) and (B) but
(C) or (D) nor

Ⓐ Ⓑ Ⓒ Ⓓ

16. The personnel office intended to interview the applicant on the 10th, but __________ she canceled due to an illness, it had to be rescheduled.

(A) while (B) although
(C) since (D) however

Ⓐ Ⓑ Ⓒ Ⓓ

17. __________ entering our assembly line, be sure to wear a safety helmet.

(A) During (B) Ever
(C) Since (D) When

Ⓐ Ⓑ Ⓒ Ⓓ

18. The hamburger steak served at that restaurant is not so tasty, __________ it is the most popular dish on the menu.

(A) because (B) yet
(C) until (D) if

Ⓐ Ⓑ Ⓒ Ⓓ

19. __________ that the meeting ends at the scheduled time, we can make it on the 5:30 bus.

(A) Suppose (B) Such
(C) Provided (D) With

Ⓐ Ⓑ Ⓒ Ⓓ

20. __________ of the Red River flood, several bridges crossing the river in Holmes County were unusable.

(A) Because (B) Yet
(C) So (D) Still

Ⓐ Ⓑ Ⓒ Ⓓ

Part 6 Text Completion

Read the text that follows. A word, phrase, or sentence is missing in parts of the text. Select the best answer to complete the text.

Questions 21-24 refer to the following announcement.

Changes to the New Jersey Railway Schedule

The following information applies to the New Jersey Railway Oceanside Express Line, which goes into service today. This new service is now _______ **21.** between Harper and Crestwood. Passengers will arrive in Crestwood in only half the time of the regular schedule: 29 minutes compared to 58 minutes. The new service stops at Billington, Jasperville and Crestwood only. For _______ **22.** of you who need Upper Rockaway Line service, you can transfer to the line at Billington. _______ **23.**. All of the trains on the Seventh Street and Upper Rockaway Lines follow the previously _______ **24.** schedules.

Fares on the Oceanside Express Line remain the same as those on the Oceanside Line. The Oceanside Express Line service operates four times an hour during the morning rush, 7:00 to 9:00, and the evening rush, 5:00 to 7:00.

21. (A) admirable
(B) available
(C) predictable
(D) touchable

Ⓐ Ⓑ Ⓒ Ⓓ

22. (A) those
(B) these
(C) there
(D) whose

Ⓐ Ⓑ Ⓒ Ⓓ

23. (A) The history of Billington Station is fascinating and complex.
(B) Billington is also the transfer point for the Seventh Street line.
(C) The Seventh Street line is no longer used.
(D) The Upper Rockaway Line is much longer than the Seventh Street Line.

Ⓐ Ⓑ Ⓒ Ⓓ

24. (A) post
(B) posting
(C) to post
(D) posted

Ⓐ Ⓑ Ⓒ Ⓓ

Read the following text. Select the best answer for each question.

Questions 25-28 refer to the following news article.

Sangershire Times-Delta Friday, 17 November 2023

Travelers prefer cruising by sea, new survey finds

A new survey released Thursday indicates that sea cruises have become more popular among travelers nationwide. Non-business air travel, on the other hand, is declining in popularity.

The British Travel Association interviewed 10,830 adult residents of Britain by phone about their leisure travel experiences and intentions. This year, 22 percent of those surveyed said they had been on a sea cruise in the previous 12 months, up from 19 percent last year.

Furthermore, 30 percent of those interviewed said they were considering taking a cruise in the coming year, compared to 25 percent the previous year.

The growing interest in cruising by sea seems to be directly linked to a declining interest in air travel. "Increased airline prices" were the number one reason mentioned by 80 percent of those who chose not to travel by plane for leisure purposes.

On the other hand, a large majority of those who have taken a sea cruise noted that "affordability" was the main factor. Other notable reasons given by respondents were the "greater convenience" and "variety of destinations available to cruise passengers."

25. What is this article mainly about?

(A) Popular sightseeing spots in Britain
(B) Trends in leisure travel
(C) A decline in travel package sales
(D) Reasons for airline ticket price increases

Ⓐ Ⓑ Ⓒ Ⓓ

26. Who answered the survey?

(A) Foreign tourists visiting Britain
(B) British travel business operators
(C) Cruise line employees
(D) People who live in Britain

Ⓐ Ⓑ Ⓒ Ⓓ

27. How many respondents might take a cruise in the next year, according to the article?

(A) 19 percent
(B) 22 percent
(C) 25 percent
(D) 30 percent

Ⓐ Ⓑ Ⓒ Ⓓ

28. Which of the following is NOT mentioned as an advantage of sea cruises?

(A) Reasonable prices
(B) Range of destinations
(C) Excellent cuisine
(D) Convenience

Ⓐ Ⓑ Ⓒ Ⓓ

Unit 12 Finance and Banking

Warm-up

Vocabulary

空欄に下から適切な語句を選んで書き入れなさい。なお、動詞については原形で記されています。必要に応じて適切な形に変えなさい。

1. If you file a tax return, you can get a ( ).
2. Please transfer $200 to our ( ) by the end of this month.
3. We don't accept ( ) larger than $50.
4. The financial experts gave us some tips on increasing our ( ) by doing some secondary jobs.
5. The seminar on investment is held every two weeks, with light ( ) usually served after the meeting.
6. People over the age of 80 prefer to deposit their money with a ( ) instead of by ATM.

refund	teller	income
refreshments	savings account	bills

TOEIC® Listening

Part 1 Photographs

You will hear four short statements. Look at the picture and choose the statement that best describes what you see in the picture.

1.

Ⓐ Ⓑ Ⓒ Ⓓ

2.

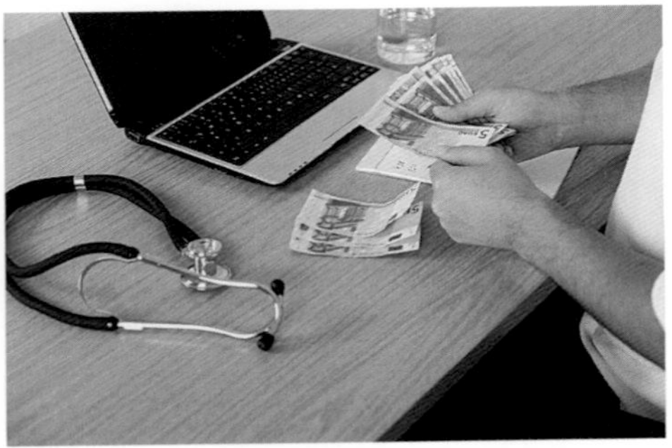

Ⓐ Ⓑ Ⓒ Ⓓ

Part 2 Question-Response 47

You will hear a question or statement and three responses. Listen carefully, and choose the best response to the question or statement.

3. Mark your answer on your answer sheet. Ⓐ Ⓑ Ⓒ

4. Mark your answer on your answer sheet. Ⓐ Ⓑ Ⓒ

5. Mark your answer on your answer sheet. Ⓐ Ⓑ Ⓒ

6. Mark your answer on your answer sheet. Ⓐ Ⓑ Ⓒ

Part 3 Conversation 48

You will hear a short conversation between two or more people. Listen carefully, and select the best response to each question.

7. What does the woman say about Jason Service Industries?
(A) It went bankrupt.
(B) It is a new company.
(C) It has many shareholders.
(D) It is financially stable.
Ⓐ Ⓑ Ⓒ Ⓓ

8. What happened to the man?
(A) He got lots of money.
(B) His investment failed.
(C) He sold some of his shares.
(D) His own company went out of business.
Ⓐ Ⓑ Ⓒ Ⓓ

9. Why did the man invest in the company?
(A) He thought the company would open new branches.
(B) He was fond of products marketed by the company.
(C) He thought the company would survive.
(D) He believed that he could sell the shares at higher price soon.
Ⓐ Ⓑ Ⓒ Ⓓ

You will hear a short talk given by a single speaker. Listen carefully, and select the best response to each question.

10. What is this program about?

(A) How to get a job
(B) How to manage company funds
(C) How much money to invest
(D) How much money to save

Ⓐ Ⓑ Ⓒ Ⓓ

11. Who is considering the possibility of being unemployed?

(A) 16% of workers
(B) 40% of workers
(C) 14% of financial experts
(D) 60% of financial experts

Ⓐ Ⓑ Ⓒ Ⓓ

12. How much is adequate savings for monthly income of $3,000?

(A) Less than $9,000
(B) More than $15,000
(C) About $12,000
(D) $50,000

Ⓐ Ⓑ Ⓒ Ⓓ

Useful Expression

Do you accept credit cards?

「クレジットカードは使えますか」という言い方です。上の言い方のほかに、Do you take credit cards? という言い方もします。Can I use a credit card? という許可を求める言い方ももちろんできますが、このように相手を主語に置いた言い方もできるようになるといいですね。

A: Do you accept credit cards?
(クレジットカードは使えますか。)

B: Of course. We accept all major credit cards.
(もちろん。主要なクレジットカードは、すべてお使いになれます。)

Grammar

前置詞

＜例題＞ 次の空所に当てはまる語句を記号で選びなさい。

① I'll call you again ___________ three days.
   (A) for　　(B) after　　(C) in　　(D) to

② You have to submit the paper ___________ the end of July.
   (A) until　　(B) for　　(C) to　　(D) by

③ This bread is so hard that you should cut it ___________ a knife.
   (A) for　　(B) by　　(C) with　　(D) of

英語母語話者は前置詞の意味を感覚としてつかんでいるため、自然と適切な前置詞が選べます。しかし、英語が母語ではない者にとっては、その感覚を十分にはつかみきれません。よく日本語の感覚に基づいて前置詞を選ぶ人がいますが、先のコラムでも書いたように、日本語の感覚と英語の感覚は必ずしも一致しているわけではないため、日本語のニュアンスのもとで英語の前置詞を選んではいけません。色々な英文を読んだり聞いたりして英語の前置詞の感覚をつかんでいくとともに、学習する際、英和辞典・英英辞典をよく引き、この動詞の後にはどのような前置詞を取るのか... などしっかりと確認していくことが必要です。

例題では、間違いやすい前置詞を取り上げました。

例題 ① は「3日後にもう一度電話します」と、これから先のことを述べていますので、「～の後」を意味する (B) afterを選んでしまうかもしれませんが、答えは (C) in です。未来のことについて「～後」という場合は、inを用いなければなりません。過去のことなら、After three days I went to Seoul.（3日後に私はソウルに行きました）のようにafterが使えます。ちなみにthree days afterという言い方はできません。I went to Seoul three days later. のように、laterを用います。

例題 ② は「～までに」の期限を示す前置詞を選ぶ必要がありますが、答えは (D) by です。(A) の untilは「～までずっと」の意味で、その時までの「継続」を示します。I was so tired that I slept until noon.（正午までずっと眠るほど私は疲れていました）のように、述部が継続を示せるものの場合はuntilを用いますが、例題 ② の場合は提出期限という「点」を示すため、byを選ばなければなりません。

例題 ③ は「～によって」の類推から、(B) byを選んだ人もいると思いますが、答えは (C) with です。「ナイフで」のような道具を示すときは前置詞withが用いられます。

（例題解答・訳）

① C（私は3日後にもう一度あなたに電話します。）
② D（あなたは7月末までに論文を提出しなければなりません。）
③ C（このパンはとても堅いので、ナイフで切らなければなりません。）

Part 5 Incomplete Sentences

A word or phrase is missing in each of the sentences below. Select the best answer to complete the sentence.

13. Liz went out to buy some refreshments for us as the vending machine was __________ order.

(A) in (B) for
(C) out of (D) right from

Ⓐ Ⓑ Ⓒ Ⓓ

14. The sales figures of Westwood Bookstores Corporation have increased __________ nearly 20 percent over last year.

(A) by (B) in
(C) for (D) to

Ⓐ Ⓑ Ⓒ Ⓓ

15. Passengers should be sure __________ check that all their travel documents are in order before proceeding to passport control.

(A) about (B) to
(C) of (D) whether

Ⓐ Ⓑ Ⓒ Ⓓ

16. The CEO has directed her energies __________ expanding the company's European market share.

(A) to (B) on
(C) with (D) by

Ⓐ Ⓑ Ⓒ Ⓓ

17. All employees are required to submit their holiday plan to their bosses __________ the end of June.

(A) in (B) to
(C) for (D) by

Ⓐ Ⓑ Ⓒ Ⓓ

18. All paperback books appearing on the national do-it-yourself bestsellers list go __________ $18.95 each.

(A) by (B) on
(C) for (D) with

Ⓐ Ⓑ Ⓒ Ⓓ

19. All the information in the customer database is stored electronically __________ a computer hard drive.

(A) into (B) to
(C) with (D) on

Ⓐ Ⓑ Ⓒ Ⓓ

20. The two partners sometimes disagree __________ details as small and unimportant as what beverages to serve at parties.

(A) between (B) about
(C) among (D) for

Ⓐ Ⓑ Ⓒ Ⓓ

Part 6 Text Completion

Read the text that follows. A word, phrase, or sentence is missing in parts of the text. Select the best answer to complete the text.

Questions 21-24 refer to the following notice.

A Service for Bank Customers

Users of Great Plains Bank can park for free in municipal St. Paul parking lots for up to three hours ------- (**21.**) day. ------- (**22.**). You need not have an account with the bank, but you do have to conduct a transaction in which money is paid. Parking ticket validation is not available for customers who only cash checks. All municipal parking lot tickets ------- (**23.**) be recognized by their blue and silver background, a picture of the Mississippi River and "ST. PAUL" in capital letters. Private parking lot tickets cannot be validated. Validation is only available ------- (**24.**) banking hours, Monday through Thursday 9:00 to 4:30, Friday 9:00 to 7:00, and Saturday 10:00 to 2:00.

21. (A) all
(B) following
(C) some
(D) each

Ⓐ Ⓑ Ⓒ Ⓓ

22. (A) Give the teller your parking ticket to be electronically validated.
(B) The parking rate is subject to change.
(C) A parking lot needs a fairly large space these days.
(D) If you would like to open an account, please follow the directions below.

Ⓐ Ⓑ Ⓒ Ⓓ

23. (A) can
(B) must
(C) will
(D) would

Ⓐ Ⓑ Ⓒ Ⓓ

24. (A) across
(B) while
(C) during
(D) beneath

Ⓐ Ⓑ Ⓒ Ⓓ

Read the following text. Select the best answer for each question.

Questions 25-28 refer to the following promotional notice.

"Investing Your Money Wisely"

Dear Concerned Investor:

CAM Assets Inc. is an asset management company that helps bring top-line investors like yourself together with various nonprofit organizations and groups that are specializing in protecting the environment, promoting education, and so many other good causes. —[1]—.

We know that you want to make the world a better place by investing your money wisely, and we help you get into the field of Socially Responsible Investing (SRI) with ease and comfort. —[2]—. We have helped many major investors to put their money where it really counts — into various projects that truly **make a difference** in society and the world. —[3]—.

Here are just a few of our biggest success stories to date:

- *$66 million invested in the Save the Amazon campaign, helping to protect sensitive rainforest areas*
- *$42 million invested in the We Are The Future project, supporting literacy in our nation's schools*
- *$25 million invested in Homes Forever, an NPO that builds affordable housing for immigrant families*

Our founder and president, the late Pete M. Camijo III, had a dream: that one day, people with lots of money would share their wealth with those who do not have much. Our founder's dream lives on at CAM Assets Inc., as we continue to dedicate ourselves to bringing those two sides together in a **win-win situation** for all.

—[4]—. Let us advise you on the most efficient ways to guide your finances into SRI. You will be truly glad you did.

CAM
Assets Inc.

4566 E. SIERRA MADRE AVENUE, SUITE 1002, FRESNO, CA. 93701
Toll-free: 1-800-253-6910

25. What field does this company help clients get into?

(A) Politically rewarding investing

(B) Socially responsible investing

(C) Legally irresponsible investing

(D) Economically unwise investing

Ⓐ Ⓑ Ⓒ Ⓓ

26. How much money has the company helped to invest in educational issues?

(A) $10 million

(B) $25 million

(C) $42 million

(D) $66 million

Ⓐ Ⓑ Ⓒ Ⓓ

27. Which kind of project would the company probably NOT get involved in?

(A) Promoting literacy in schools

(B) Supporting immigrant families

(C) Preserving natural areas

(D) Developing downtown areas with more skyscrapers

Ⓐ Ⓑ Ⓒ Ⓓ

28. In which of the positions marked [1], [2], [3], and [4] does the following sentence best belong?

"Won't you join us in making this dream a reality for your investment funds as well?"

(A) [1]

(B) [2]

(C) [3]

(D) [4]

Ⓐ Ⓑ Ⓒ Ⓓ

Unit 13 Media

Warm-up

Vocabulary

空欄に下から適切な語句を選んで書き入れなさい。なお、動詞については原形で記されています。必要に応じて適切な形に変えなさい。

1. The regular (　　　　　　) of this electronics retail store have membership ID cards.
2. The (　　　　　　) period for the new personal computer is five years after the purchase.
3. XP37, the most popular office printer, often has problems with paper (　　　　　　) and the company started recalling the product this Monday.
4. Major electronics stores usually offer free (　　　　　　) service within three months after your purchase.
5. The morning news says the trains are delayed (　　　　　　) heavy snow.
6. The news report says that the volcanic explosion has caused some cuts in water (　　　　　　).

supply	warranty	due to
clients	repair	jams

TOEIC® Listening

Part 1 Photographs

50

You will hear four short statements. Look at the picture and choose the statement that best describes what you see in the picture.

1.

Ⓐ Ⓑ Ⓒ Ⓓ

2.

Ⓐ Ⓑ Ⓒ Ⓓ

Part 2 Question-Response 51

You will hear a question or statement and three responses. Listen carefully, and choose the best response to the question or statement.

3. Mark your answer on your answer sheet. Ⓐ Ⓑ Ⓒ

4. Mark your answer on your answer sheet. Ⓐ Ⓑ Ⓒ

5. Mark your answer on your answer sheet. Ⓐ Ⓑ Ⓒ

6. Mark your answer on your answer sheet. Ⓐ Ⓑ Ⓒ

Part 3 Conversation 52

You will hear a short conversation between two or more people. Listen carefully, and select the best response to each question.

7. What is indicated about the meetings?
(A) They will be held three days a week.
(B) They will be held at the office and online.
(C) Board members are to set the date.
(D) Employees do not have to attend them. Ⓐ Ⓑ Ⓒ Ⓓ

8. What can the employees do from next month?
(A) Reduce the burden of housework
(B) Take three days off
(C) Buy a new software security package
(D) Attend online meetings Ⓐ Ⓑ Ⓒ Ⓓ

9. What does the man mean when he says, "I can use my spare time more effectively"?
(A) The employees don't need to go to work.
(B) The employees can do some other things.
(C) The employees have to work more.
(D) The employees can save money for their families. Ⓐ Ⓑ Ⓒ Ⓓ

Part 4 Talk 53

You will hear a short talk given by a single speaker. Listen carefully, and select the best response to each question.

10. Who uses this printer?

(A) Office workers
(B) Individuals
(C) The manufacturer of ZW90
(D) Technicians

Ⓐ Ⓑ Ⓒ Ⓓ

11. What is NOT mentioned in this announcement?

(A) The printer's speed
(B) The cost of the paper
(C) After-purchase servicing
(D) Electricity consumption

Ⓐ Ⓑ Ⓒ Ⓓ

12. How long is the guarantee period?

(A) Eight hours
(B) Ninety days
(C) Five years
(D) Seven years

Ⓐ Ⓑ Ⓒ Ⓓ

Useful Expression

Kate is hooked on TV dramas.

「ケイトはテレビドラマに夢中になっています」という意味です。"hook" はもともと「引っかける」とか「留める」という意味ですが、そこから派生して「夢中にさせる」という意味が生まれ、"be hooked on ～" で「～に夢中になる」という意味が出てきました。こういう少しくだけた口語表現も覚えておくといいですね。

A: Kate is really hooked on TV dramas. She always talks about the plots and characters of the dramas.
（ケイトはテレビドラマに本当に夢中になってるよ。いつもドラマの筋書きや登場人物について話してるからね。）

B: I know. She records all the shows and watches them over and over.
（そうだね。彼女はドラマを全て録画して、何度も何度も観ているよ。）

Grammar

語彙

TOEIC® L&RのPart 5には、これまで見てきた文法問題だけではなく、適切な語句を選ぶ語彙問題もあります。中には文法的には選択肢 (A) から (D) のどれでも当てはまるものもあり、文法的見地からではなく、語彙として一番しっくりくるものを選び抜く術が必要になります。

語彙問題は様々な形があり、一筋縄ではいきませんが、その一つとしてコロケーション（語と語のつながり）に関する問題が出ることがあります。例えば、日本語の「する」に対応する英語は何かと尋ねられれば、皆さんは何と答えますか。"do" と答える人も多いと思います。確かに do one's homework（宿題をする）、do the dishes（皿洗いをする）のようにdoを取るものも多いですが、have a meal（食事する）、play baseball（野球する）、make a mistake（失敗する）のようにdo以外の動詞を使う例も多数あります。do a meal, do baseball, do a mistakeという言い方はできません。

日頃からこのようなコロケーションに目を配るようにしておくことも重要です。

TOEIC® Reading

Part 5 Incomplete Sentences

A word or phrase is missing in each of the sentences below. Select the best answer to complete the sentence.

13. The firm is facing a serious cash crisis and it is set to __________ bankrupt by the end of this year.

(A) make (B) do
(C) get (D) go

Ⓐ Ⓑ Ⓒ Ⓓ

14. Comparing the cost of oil and natural gas, the __________ is usually more affordable than the former in this country.

(A) latter (B) later
(C) last (D) latest

Ⓐ Ⓑ Ⓒ Ⓓ

15. Doctors generally __________ much more money than nurses, while the hours they work are not so different.

(A) earn (B) are
(C) take (D) work

Ⓐ Ⓑ Ⓒ Ⓓ

16. Easston Stanley offers a __________ range of investment services to fulfill the individual needs of its clients.

(A) long (B) far
(C) high (D) wide

Ⓐ Ⓑ Ⓒ Ⓓ

17. The United States has recently started allowing American companies to __________ business with Cuba on a limited basis.

(A) give (B) do
(C) make (D) run

Ⓐ Ⓑ Ⓒ Ⓓ

18. The troubles of the audio system and the microphones of the conference room have forced us to postpone the workshop for a __________.

(A) bit (B) now
(C) short (D) future

Ⓐ Ⓑ Ⓒ Ⓓ

19. The host of the show could not __________ the name of the guest in the middle of the program.

(A) know (B) remind
(C) teach (D) recall

Ⓐ Ⓑ Ⓒ Ⓓ

20. Considering all the work the committee was given at the last minute, can they __________ to finish it all before the deadline?

(A) do (B) manage
(C) complete (D) achieve

Ⓐ Ⓑ Ⓒ Ⓓ

Part 6 Text Completion

Read the text that follows. A word, phrase, or sentence is missing in parts of the text. Select the best answer to complete the text.

Questions 21-24 refer to the following letter.

Dear Ms. Kingsley,

Thank you for your article about your trip to Thailand. Unfortunately, we published an article on that _______ topic just four months ago. It is our policy never to cover the same topic twice within any 12-month period.
21.

The style and content of the article, however, were exactly what "Explorations" is looking for. I would like to encourage you to _______ a different article about another of your travels.
22.
_______. One of your many other trips could easily be the material for an interesting article. To assist you, I have included a list of all topics we have covered in the last 10 months and the two issues that will come out in the near future.
23.

_______ you start writing, give me a call at (871) 903-5386 so we can talk about your topic, the schedule, procedures for editing and payment. Typically, we prefer articles that are 1,000 words long with three to five photos per article.
24.

Sincerely,

Deborah McFadden

Assistant Editor, *Explorations* magazine

21. (A) very
(B) sure
(C) sort
(D) well

Ⓐ Ⓑ Ⓒ Ⓓ

22. (A) transpire
(B) entertain
(C) submit
(D) converse

Ⓐ Ⓑ Ⓒ Ⓓ

23. (A) Your travel experiences are not so attractive to us.
(B) We believe that traveling overseas may change your future lifestyle.
(C) We understand that you are well-traveled.
(D) Traveling is not the main theme of the next issue of our magazine.

Ⓐ Ⓑ Ⓒ Ⓓ

24. (A) Upon
(B) Before
(C) Within
(D) Against

Ⓐ Ⓑ Ⓒ Ⓓ

Read the following texts. Select the best answer for each question.

Questions 25-29 refer to the following review and e-mail.

My 5 Million-Dollar Loss by Alberto Allende

Reviewed by: Carmen Boric

Books about running a successful business are a dime a dozen, but you don't expect a book entitled *My 5 Million-Dollar Loss* to be about success. However, Alberto Allende's fascinating book is, ultimately, about just that. He examines why his initial jewelry business flopped and how he used this unfortunate experience to flourish in his second attempt.

Mr. Allende started out as a part-time salesman in a cellphone shop. He found that most customers threw away their old phones and realized he could extract materials like gold, copper and silver from these devices. So, Mr. Allende opened a small business making and selling jewelry made of those extracted components. Throughout the book, Mr. Allende shares with readers every mistake he made in his business. "My idea was great, but I lacked research," he says. Eventually, though, through hard work and a flexible attitude, Mr. Allende proved his idea was a good one and has expanded into several countries.

It is a refreshing and educational story that teaches readers the right time to give up or change plans. It provides excellent insights on overspending and failing to take advantage of e-commerce or online shopping sites. For people who have just kick-started their business, this book by Alberto Allende is a must-read!

To: Alberto Allende <alberto_allende@authorsclub.net>
From: Marsha Sanders <M.Sanders@moonstonepublishing.com>
Subject: Book Event
Date: Friday, 28 April 2023

Dear Mr. Allende,

My name is Marsha Sanders, and I work for the events division of Moonstone Publishing. Congratulations on the great reviews your book is getting so far!

I received a speaking request from Mr. Timothy Wein, a business lecturer at Cornel Western University and a small business owner. He is a big fan of your book and would like you to speak at his university's upcoming "Modern Business Problems Forum". If you could share more about your book and about your business, his students will greatly appreciate it.

The forum is in July, but would you be free next week to discuss the event's program in detail with Mr. Wein? Looking forward to hearing from you.

Kind regards,
Marsha Sanders

25. What is Mr. Allende's business?

(A) Buying second-hand cellphones and selling them
(B) Mending broken pieces of jewelry
(C) Selling jewelry made from recycled materials
(D) Selling pieces of gold from unwanted cellphones

Ⓐ Ⓑ Ⓒ Ⓓ

26. According to Ms. Boric, who is the book recommended for?

(A) Aspiring authors
(B) New business owners
(C) Part-time workers
(D) University students

Ⓐ Ⓑ Ⓒ Ⓓ

27. Why is Ms. Sanders contacting Mr. Allende?

(A) To ask him to write another book
(B) To encourage him to try e-commerce
(C) To inform him of an invitation
(D) To invite him to attend a lecture

Ⓐ Ⓑ Ⓒ Ⓓ

28. What do Mr. Allende and Mr. Wein have in common?

(A) Both are authors of business books.
(B) Both are lecturers at a university.
(C) Both have lost a large amount of money.
(D) Both have owned a small business.

Ⓐ Ⓑ Ⓒ Ⓓ

29. What does Ms. Sanders want Mr. Allende to talk about next week?

(A) How to gain more positive book reviews
(B) Other events with Moonstone Publishing
(C) The forum's agenda with Mr. Wein
(D) The payment details for giving a speech

Ⓐ Ⓑ Ⓒ Ⓓ

Unit 14

Health and Welfare

Warm-up

Vocabulary

空欄に下から適切な語句を選んで書き入れなさい。なお、動詞については原形で記されています。必要に応じて適切な形に変えなさい。

1. The hospital is filled with ( ) patients, and doctors and nurses wear masks to avoid infection.
2. I have some hesitation to take ( ) today because I have an important meeting with one of my clients.
3. Children under age three have to receive ( ) against major infectious diseases.
4. In Japan, people are required to join a ( ) system and pay some premiums every month.
5. To ( ) the opening of the new City Medical Center, some special events are being planned.
6. Every family doctor and general hospital asks patients for a first-visit ( ).

health insurance	celebrate	fee	flu	vaccinations	sick leave

TOEIC® Listening

Part 1 Photographs

You will hear four short statements. Look at the picture and choose the statement that best describes what you see in the picture.

1.

Ⓐ Ⓑ Ⓒ Ⓓ

2.

Ⓐ Ⓑ Ⓒ Ⓓ

Part 2 Question-Response

55

You will hear a question or statement and three responses. Listen carefully, and choose the best response to the question or statement.

3. Mark your answer on your answer sheet. (A) (B) (C)

4. Mark your answer on your answer sheet. (A) (B) (C)

5. Mark your answer on your answer sheet. (A) (B) (C)

6. Mark your answer on your answer sheet. (A) (B) (C)

56

You will hear a short conversation between two or more people. Listen carefully, and select the best response to each question.

7. Why is the man not feeling well?

(A) He is under stress at work.
(B) He went to see his sister.
(C) Last month was the busiest time of the year.
(D) He has to make a big decision by himself. (A) (B) (C) (D)

8. What does the man have to do?

(A) Cover for his co-worker while he's away
(B) Go to Sydney for Sam
(C) Get some medicine for the woman
(D) Make a business trip (A) (B) (C) (D)

9. What does the woman recommend the man to do?

(A) Get enough sleep
(B) Tell his boss about the problem
(C) Go on a diet
(D) Consider nutritional balance (A) (B) (C) (D)

You will hear a short talk given by a single speaker. Listen carefully, and select the best response to each question.

10. What does the ODC recommend the listeners to do?

(A) Get a shot
(B) Take some medicine
(C) Get a medical check
(D) Write a doctor's certificate

Ⓐ Ⓑ Ⓒ Ⓓ

11. Why do medical institutions have to conduct targeted vaccinations?

(A) The number of patients is increasing.
(B) There will not be enough flu vaccine.
(C) The holiday season starts soon.
(D) Doctors are taking vacations.

Ⓐ Ⓑ Ⓒ Ⓓ

12. According to the announcement, who are in the "at-risk group"?

(A) People in their 30s
(B) All patients
(C) Children
(D) Teenagers

Useful Expression

What's wrong?

「どうかしましたか」という言い方で、落ち込んでいたり、具合が悪そうな人に掛けることばです。人だけではなく、"What's wrong with this fridge?"（この冷蔵庫、どうしたのかな）のように、物に対しても用いることができます。

A: What's wrong with you? You looked depressed during the meeting.
（どうしたんだ。会議中、ずっと落ち込んでいるように見えたけど。）

B: Yeah, I made terrible mistakes, and my client got very angry. I've been thinking about how I should fix the relationship with him.
（ああ、ひどいミスをして、依頼人がとても怒ったんだ。どうやって彼と関係を修復しようかと考えているんだよ。）

TOEIC® Reading

Part 5 Incomplete Sentences

A word or phrase is missing in each of the sentences below. Select the best answer to complete the sentence.

13. Every deal I proposed went through __________ smoothly that I'm beginning to wonder if the board members were really paying close attention to the details.

(A) so (B) very
(C) such (D) well

Ⓐ Ⓑ Ⓒ Ⓓ

14. To transfer funds to your savings account, you may move funds either from your primary checking account __________ from an account at another institution.

(A) and (B) or
(C) but (D) nor

Ⓐ Ⓑ Ⓒ Ⓓ

15. Of all the groups asked about the product's design, the survey shows it is __________ appealing to young professionals.

(A) very (B) such
(C) much (D) most

Ⓐ Ⓑ Ⓒ Ⓓ

16. The spokesperson for the government had to __________ the minister's speech when news arrived of the fire at the train station.

(A) intervene (B) intersect
(C) interrupt (D) interpret

Ⓐ Ⓑ Ⓒ Ⓓ

17. Construction of new homes has increased sharply in the last year, reflecting not only growth in that industry __________ also an upturn in the economy.

(A) and (B) therefore
(C) but (D) thus

Ⓐ Ⓑ Ⓒ Ⓓ

18. If you are looking for work, it is __________ checking the advertisements in the newspaper.

(A) important (B) worth
(C) necessary (D) valuable

Ⓐ Ⓑ Ⓒ Ⓓ

19. The job will go to the candidate __________ knowledge of the industry is the broadest.

(A) who (B) whom
(C) whose (D) whoever

Ⓐ Ⓑ Ⓒ Ⓓ

20. The speaker's voice was so small and trembling that I could __________ understand the presentation.

(A) easily (B) ever
(C) hardly (D) nothing

Ⓐ Ⓑ Ⓒ Ⓓ

Part 6 Text Completion

Read the text that follows. A word, phrase, or sentence is missing in parts of the text. Select the best answer to complete the text.

Questions 21-24 refer to the following article.

Most people are not getting enough sleep, specialists say, and the problems that result are apparent — and potentially serious.

"Absenteeism, 'presenteeism'— people showing up for work really tired — car accidents, medical errors," said Elizabeth Klerman, a Massachusetts General Hospital sleep expert and professor of neurology at Harvard Medical School. "There are -------(**21.**) effects on mood, psychiatric disorders, cardiovascular disorders, increased obesity, probably cancer, definitely dementia and neurologic diseases."

As is often the case with many problems rooted in behavior, the first step is acknowledging the problem.

Numerous studies have shown that most of us don't sleep enough to be -------(**22.**) and that long-term deprivation carries significant health ills. But while most of us understand that -------(**23.**) rest is an important factor in personal health, we still treat a good night's sleep as a luxury — even an oddity — settling instead for what we've convinced ourselves is enough to "get by."

"-------(**24.**). Most people are not getting enough sleep overall," Klerman said. "Don't worry about whether your schedule is regular, if you're not usually getting enough sleep."

21. (A) sedative
(B) adverse
(C) beneficial
(D) subtle

Ⓐ Ⓑ Ⓒ Ⓓ

22. (A) rest
(B) rests
(C) resting
(D) rested

Ⓐ Ⓑ Ⓒ Ⓓ

23. (A) adequate
(B) scarce
(C) tentative
(D) excessive

Ⓐ Ⓑ Ⓒ Ⓓ

24. (A) People should also keep the same sleeping hours on weekends.
(B) As the saying goes, the early bird catches the worm.
(C) We encourage people to get more sleep on nights when they don't have work or school the next day.
(D) There's a disconnect between how alert people feel and how much sleep they get.

Ⓐ Ⓑ Ⓒ Ⓓ

Part 7 Multiple Passages

Read the following texts. Select the best answer for each question.

Questions 25-29 refer to the following flyer and form.

BODY FIT

SPORTS AND FITNESS CENTER

To celebrate our three-year anniversary in July, **BODY FIT** is offering a special promotional membership price for new members. Sign up anytime next month at **BODY FIT** and save $100 on a one-year membership!

Membership includes:

- Unlimited use of gym equipment and facilities
- Safe, effective and personalized programs for weight loss and strength training
- Friendly, helpful and qualified advice
- Weekly classes with qualified instructors:
  Aerobics with Sasha Mellon ▪ Yoga with Sardit Patel
  Water Aerobics with Penelope Hyde ▪ Zumba with Latonya Delfino
  ...and more!
- Bath, whirlpool and sauna facilities

And available for an additional fee:

- Massage service by licensed physical therapist
- Tanning equipment

Monthly memberships are available for as low as $79.95 per month.
Contact **BODY FIT** on the reverse side for details!

BODY FIT

SPORTS AND FITNESS CENTER

MEMBERS FEEDBACK FORM

Dear New Member,

We welcome your feedback and encourage you to take the time to fill out this form. Your comments will help us to provide you with the best possible services in the future.

	Excellent	Good	Satisfactory	Poor
➤ Staff Courtesy	☑	☐	☐	☐
➤ Atmosphere	☑	☐	☐	☐
➤ Cleanliness of Facilities	☑	☐	☐	☐
➤ Quality of Equipment	☐	☑	☐	☐
➤ Quality of Classes	☐	☐	☑	☐
➤ Membership Fee	☐	☐	☐	☑

➤ Staff Courtesy
Comment: *Personable and always pleasant to talk to.*

➤ Atmosphere
Comment: *Comfortable. There are people of all types, ages, interests here.*

➤ Cleanliness of Facilities
Comment: *Spotless and immaculate bath and change areas - thank you!*

➤ Quality of Equipment
Comment: *In good condition. The range could be a little more diverse.*

➤ Quality of Classes
Comment: *With the exception of Latonya Delfino, I was not very impressed with the instructors overall.*

➤ Membership Fee
Comment: *Too expensive! More of my friends would join if the price came down a little.*

25. What service is available for an additional charge?

(A) Yoga classes
(B) Sauna
(C) Massage
(D) Personal training

Ⓐ Ⓑ Ⓒ Ⓓ

26. What limit is placed on the discount offer?

(A) It is for current members only.
(B) It is valid for three-year memberships only.
(C) It does not include participation in classes.
(D) It is only offered to people who sign up next month.

Ⓐ Ⓑ Ⓒ Ⓓ

27. What is indicated about weight loss programs offered at Body Fit?

(A) They include unlimited use of the training facilities.
(B) They are adapted to meet individual needs.
(C) They are not convenient for members.
(D) They require a doctor's permission to participate.

Ⓐ Ⓑ Ⓒ Ⓓ

28. Which class did the customer appreciate the most?

(A) Yoga
(B) Aerobics
(C) Water Aerobics
(D) Zumba

Ⓐ Ⓑ Ⓒ Ⓓ

29. According to the survey form, how could Body Fit improve its services?

(A) By installing a wider variety of equipment
(B) By holding longer classes
(C) By hiring friendlier employees
(D) By moving to a more convenient location

Ⓐ Ⓑ Ⓒ Ⓓ

一歩上を目指す TOEIC®L&R TEST: Level 3 [二訂版]

検印省略

©2017年1月31日　第1版発行
2022年1月31日　第8刷発行
2024年1月31日　二訂版第1版発行

編著者　北尾　泰幸
西田　晴美
林　姿穂
Brian Covert

発行者　小川　洋一郎
発行所　株式会社 朝日出版社
〒101-0065 東京都千代田区西神田3-3-5
電話　東京　(03) 3239-0271
FAX　東京　(03) 3239-0479
E-mail　text-e@asahipress.com
振替口座　00140-2-46008
https://www.asahipress.com/
組版／メディアアート　製版／錦明印刷

乱丁・落丁本はお取り替えいたします。
ISBN 978-4-255-15721-4